# SEVEN HINDRANCES
# TO THE BLESSINGS OF GOD

## Identifying and Removing Hindrances to Spiritual Growth and God's Blessings

### Jamal E. Quinn

I0087567

# Table of Contents

Dedication............................................................4

Introduction..........................................................5

1. What God really intended for us..........................6

2. Disobedience....................................................20

3. Idolatry...........................................................43

4. Pride..............................................................60

5. Rebellion........................................................72

6. Unbelief..........................................................86

7. Unforgiveness.................................................103

8. Unrepentance.................................................112

References.........................................................126

About the Author................................................127

# DEDICATION

This book is dedicated to my late parents Leslie Thomas and Mary Lillian Quinn, and to my late grandparents Deacon Leroy and Eddie Mae Downs who were wonderful Saints in the LORD. They were a great example to me when I was young, and showed me the love of Christ, instilling in me unwavering faith.

I am eternally thankful and grateful for their inspiration, encouragement, and love. To my beautiful and wonderful wife of my youth; Sheryl, who has stood beside me with unceasing , sincere dedication for 21 years of military service, and many years of marriage. Thank you for being a loving and supportive wife! All that we have accomplished together is only because of God's grace, favor and abundant blessings!

To my daughter Jamika, Son-In-Law Corby and Granddaughter Cadence who have been a blessing to me in so many ways, thank you for your sincere dedication and support. To all of the faithful Firm Foundation members, who have labored and served faithfully unto the LORD, thank you for your servitude and service in Jesus Name!

# INTRODUCTION

For many years it has been in my heart to write this book. It began as a teaching series many years ago as I taught the people of God about hindrances to the blessings of God. As we explored and expounded the scriptures, I began to see a pattern from the Old Testament to the New Testament where the Lord blessed his obedient saints who embraced his precious promises in the Word. There were others who did not abide in his Word, hindering the blessing that God desired to pour out upon them.

These hindrances often caused the Lord to discipline them or to remove his divine protection from them for a season. Once they confessed their sin and repented there was restoration. The Bible says that Jesus Christ is the same yesterday, today and forever more. (Hebrews 13: 8) Although we live in an age of grace, the spirit of disobedience, idolatry, rebellion, unbelief, unforgiveness and unrepentance still abounds among many, hindering the blessing that God desires to pour out upon his people.

Although we are a New Testament church, and God in his great grace causes the rain to fall on the righteous and the unrighteous, true blessing is reserved for his obedient children who are not only hearers but doers of the Word! (James 1: 22). We must endeavor to follow the example of our Lord Jesus Christ, who did no sin nor was deceit found in his mouth according to 1 Peter 2: 21-22.

# CHAPTER 1 - WHAT GOD REALLY INTENDED FOR US

"So, God created man in His own image; in the image of God He created him; male and female He created them. **Then God blessed them** and God said to them, "Be fruitful and multiply; fill the earth and subdue it; have dominion over the fish of the sea, over the birds of the air, and over every living thing that moves on the earth." "Genesis 1:27-28 NKJV"

As we look intently into the scriptures we find that from the beginning of time with our first parents in the Garden of Eden, God bestowed a blessing on Adam and Eve. It has always been the will of the Father to bless his beloved creation in the earth with the blessings of heaven, but because of sin and man's disobedience, God in his infinite wisdom did two things. He removed them from the Garden of Eden and disciplined them for their disobedience.

"So, the LORD God said to the serpent: "Because you have done this, you are cursed more than all cattle, and more than every beast of the field; on your belly you shall go, and you shall eat dust All the days of your life." Genesis 3:14 NKJV

"Therefore, the LORD God sent him out of the Garden of Eden to till the ground from which he was taken." Genesis 3:23 NKJV

We must understand that God is eternal, holy, righteous and true. Sin cannot dwell in his presence, so we must come before him on His terms to receive forgiveness of sin, restoration and blessing. As earthly parents we all have children whom we love with all of our hearts. Even in their waywardness, when they did something wrong we disciplined them, but our love never left them. Although there were hindrances on their behalf that caused us to withhold the blessing until they apologized, and exercised forgiveness for the wrongdoing.  It is always our desire to bless our children, but the blessing that we bestow on them as parents is on our terms and not their terms!

As it is in the natural, so it is in the spiritual. Our wonderful heavenly Father loves us and desires to bless us high and above measure, but it is on his terms and not our terms.
The Lord desires that we as obedient children walk according to his Holy Word. In order for us to receive the true blessings of salvation made possible through the blood of Jesus Christ, it is on his terms and not our terms. I believe that the greatest blessing that one can receive is accepting Jesus Christ as Lord and Savior.

So, as we journey through the scriptures to discuss *Seven Hindrances to the Blessings of God*, let's first define hindrance and blessing!  Hindrance can be defined as the act of hindering. The condition of being hindered, or something that hinders. It is also an impediment, obstruction, snag or the act of hindering or prevention. Blessing can be defined as the act of invoking divine protection or aid. It is approval, good wishes or the bestowal of a divine gift or favor.
When we look at our lives and everything that the Lord has done for us, we can truly say that we are a blessed people. The Lord has bestowed upon us grace, mercy and favor, and we can truly say that the Lord is good and his mercy endures forever. (Psalm 107: 1).

The Lord has blessed us abundantly as the people of God and as a nation. Yet, in these last days our society has increased with violence, hate, immorality, materialism, uncertainty, terrorism and war. All of these things are a result of sin and wickedness in the hearts of men caused by disobedience, idolatry, pride, rebellion, unbelief, unforgiveness and an unrepentant heart. In the beginning when God created the heavens and the earth, this was by no stretch of the imagination what God had purposed for his beloved creation. When we read Gen 1:27-31, it states:

Genesis 1:27-31 NKJV
27 So God created man in His own image; in the image of God, He created him; male and female He created them.
28 Then God blessed them, and God said to them, "Be fruitful and multiply; fill the earth and subdue it; have dominion over the fish of the sea, over the birds of the air, and over every living thing that moves on the earth."
29 And God said, "See, I have given you every herb that yields seed which is on the face of all the earth, and every tree whose fruit yields seed; to you it shall be for food.
30 Also, to every beast of the earth, to every bird of the air, and to everything that creeps on the earth, in which there is life, I have given every green herb for food"; and it was so.
31 Then God saw everything that He had made, and indeed it was very good. So, the evening and the morning were the sixth day.

   The Bible states that God created man in his image (verse 27). In (verse 28) it also says that God blessed them. In other words, they were created in the image of a righteous, holy, loving God who blessed them with everything that they would ever need in the garden. They had it all. They had no need of anything.

   They had dominion and charge of everything in the garden. They had every seed they needed to produce and grow food (verse 29). He gave them charge of the beasts of the field, fowl of the air and every creeping thing on the earth and green plants for food. (verse 30). As a matter of fact, God was excited about his creation because the Bible says in (verse 31), "God saw everything that he had made, and behold it was very good."

I can understand why God was excited because everything that he created was perfect, a work of art and a masterpiece, which was very good. Think of this in human terms. When we complete a task that turns out to be exceptionally good, we would probably take a look at the end result and say, "Wow, this looks great, or this is awesome!

I believe that God took great pleasure in what he had created. It was his master creation. Man and woman created in his image, a chip off the old block.
He would be their God and they would be his creation. Fellowshipping in the garden, having a grand of a time enjoying them and in turn they would worship and love him forever.  They had everything they would ever need and all these things and more were part of the blessing of God upon their lives.
They had no need of anything, nor desired anything. They had fellowship with the Almighty, the Creator, the Ancient of Days, the Everlasting Father of Heaven and Earth.

They were truly blessed, but one day something terrible happened! Adam and Eve were spending time enjoying the Garden of Eden, and one another as God had purposed for them. Yet, something extremely bad happened that has reverberated down through the ages for thousands of years to this day causing men and women to fall short of the Glory of God. They disobeyed the commandment of God.

We must understand that God gave Adam a commandment, but he also gave him liberty to partake of everything in the garden except that which he was told not to eat.

"And the LORD God commanded the man, saying, "Of every tree of the garden you may freely eat." (Gen 2:16) "But of the tree of the knowledge of good and evil you shall not eat, for in the day that you eat of it you shall surely die." (Gen 2:17)

So, we find that the blessing that was bestowed upon them was contingent upon their obedience to the commandment of the Lord!

## The Origination of Sin

So, we find in Genesis Chap 3: 1-11, the origination of sin in which the Bible says:

Genesis 3:1-11 NKJV
1 Now the serpent was more cunning than any beast of the field which the LORD God had made. And he said to the woman, "Has God indeed said, 'You shall not eat of every tree of the garden'?"
2 And the woman said to the serpent, "We may eat the fruit of the trees of the garden;
3 but of the fruit of the tree which is in the midst of the garden, God has said, 'You shall not eat it, nor shall you touch it, lest you die.' "
4 Then the serpent said to the woman, "You will not surely die.
5 For God knows that in the day you eat of it your eyes will be opened, and you will be like God, knowing good and evil."
6 So when the woman saw that the tree was good for food, that it was pleasant to the eyes, and a tree desirable to make one wise, she took of its fruit and ate. She also gave to her husband with her, and he ate.
7 Then the eyes of both of them were opened, and they knew that they were naked; and they sewed fig leaves

together and made themselves coverings.

8 And they heard the sound of the LORD God walking in the garden in the cool of the day, and Adam and his wife hid themselves from the presence of the LORD God among the trees of the garden.

9 Then the LORD God called to Adam and said to him, "Where are you?"

10 So he said, "I heard your voice in the garden, and I was afraid because I was naked; and I hid myself."

11 And He said, "Who told you that you were naked? Have you eaten from the tree of which I commanded you that you should not eat?"

What caused Adam and Even to hide from God? What caused them to lose fellowship with God? What caused God to be so angry with them? What caused them to be banished from the Garden of Eden and the presence of God?

First and foremost, we can see that deception by Satan and disobedience to the commandment (Word) of God caused them to fall out of fellowship with God, and opened the door to sin. Satan has been deceiving the nations of people for thousands of years causing them to disobey the Holy commandments and the Word of God. Satan has also deceived the world into believing the big lie.  The deceptive lie that God doesn't care for us, that he allows bad things to happen to good people, and that he doesn't want us to enjoy the blessings of life. We know that this is a complete lie.  For the Bible says that Satan is a murderer and the father of lies:

"You are of the Devil as father, and the lusts of your father you will do. He was a murderer from the beginning, and did not abide in the truth because there is no truth in him. When he speaks a lie, he speaks of his own, for he is a liar and the father of it." John 8:44 NKJV

Jesus tells us that the Devil is the Father of lies and that he comes to steal, kill and to destroy. This stealing, killing and destruction from the evil one has created hindrances to the blessing of God through sin. Jesus said it like this:

"The thief does not come except to steal, and to kill, and to destroy. I have come that they may have life, and that they may have it more abundantly."
John 10:10 NKJV

God loves us so much that he sent his only son to die for us and to redeem us from the curse of the law of sin and death. God has truly blessed us and his commandments are to keep us from hurt, harm and danger.

Satan uses deceptive devices against us to get us out of fellowship with God. His desire is to deceive and hinder us, so that we will not experience the abundant life that God has purposed for us.

**The Definition of Sin**

When we talk about hindrances to the blessings of God, we are referring to sin. So, what is sin? The definition of sin is: Lawlessness or a missing of the mark, perversity, transgression, to miss the mark, or injustice. The practical definition of sin is disobedience to the law of God or the Word of God.

1 John 3: 4 describes it this way: "Everyone who practices sin also practices lawlessness, for sin is lawlessness."

Sin is rampant in the world today, and many people have forsaken truth to embrace the lie of the enemy. When I first came to know Christ, the LORD gave me a

scripture which can be found in Proverbs 14: 12 and
Proverbs 16: 25:
"There is a way that seems right to a man, but its end is
the way of death."
Proverbs 14:12 NKJV

"There is a way that seem s right to a man, but its end is
the way of death."
Proverbs 16:25 NKJV

Can you imagine going through life thinking you are
right and be totally wrong?
Many people in the world today continue to believe the
lie that was told by Satan which caused Adam and Eve to
sin against God. The Devil is still asking that same
question: "Did God really say?" The answer to that
question is yes, God did say, and Jesus echoed this in his
word:

"If ye love me, keep my commandments."
John 14:15 KJV

"Jesus answered and said unto him, if a man loves me,
he will keep my words: and my Father will love him, and
we will come unto him, and make our abode with him."
John 14:23 KJV

"He who does not love me does not keep My Words, and
the Word which you hear is not mine, but the Fathers
who sent me."
John 14: 24 NKJV

The Bible says if we truly love the Lord Jesus Christ and
one another, we will keep his commandments.

"By this we know that we love the children of God, when
we love God and keep His commandments. For this is
the love of God, that we keep His commandments, and

His commandments are not burdensome."
1 John 5:2-3 NKJV

The sin of disobedience was the problem in the garden. They did not keep God's commandments and it caused them to fall short of God's Glory, and they were evicted from the Garden.

## The Seven Hindrances

The important thing to remember is that God's wonderful grace sustains all who repent and call upon his majestic name. We must recognize that it is the enemy's desires to deceive and prevent us from receiving all that God purposed for us through his glorious grace and wonderful blessings. We must also remember that God hates sin but loves the sinner. He loves us, but he does not like the sin in us. The seven hindrances to the blessing of God are a reminder that God will not tolerate sin, evil or wickedness.

The seven hindrances are recorded in scripture throughout the Bible from Genesis to Revelation, and have caused men and women throughout the ages to fall short of the glory of God.
These hindrances have also hindered them from having a fruitful and blessed relationship with the Most High God. Thereby, missing the mark and hindering the blessing of God that he desires to pour out upon his people. The seven hindrances are behaviors and attitudes manifested through sin and perpetuated by evil and demonic spirits. Their goal is to hinder our relationship with God, and to cause us to fall out of fellowship with God, and they are:

**1. Disobedience**
**2. Idolatry**
**3. Pride**

**4. Rebellion**
**5. Unbelief**
**6. Unforgiveness**
**7. Unrepentance**

Throughout the Bible, especially in the Old Testament, we find many examples where the saints pleased and displeased God. As a matter of fact, we read in many Old Testament books some people did right in the sight of the LORD, and others did evil in the sight of the Lord. Those that were obedient and followed the commandments of God received the blessings of God, and those that disobeyed the Word of God were disciplined.

In 1 Corinthians 10: 1-12, the scriptures admonish us to adhere to the examples of those that came before us.

(1) Moreover, brethren, I do not want you to be unaware that all our fathers were under the cloud, all passed through the sea,
(2) All were baptized into Moses in the cloud and in the sea,
(3) All ate the same spiritual food,
(4) and all drank the same spiritual drink. For they drank of that spiritual Rock that followed them, and that Rock was Christ.
(5) But with most of them God was not well pleased, for their bodies were scattered in the wilderness.
(6) Now these things became our examples, to the intent that we should not lust after evil things as they also lusted.
(7) And do not become idolaters as were some of them. As it is written, "The people sat down to eat and drink, and rose up to play."
(8) Nor let us commit sexual immorality, as some of them did, and in one day twenty-three thousand fell;
(9) Nor let us tempt Christ, as some of them also

tempted, and were destroyed by serpents;

(10) Nor complain, as some of them also complained, and were destroyed by the destroyer.

(11) **Now all these things happened to them as examples, and they were written for our admonition, upon whom the ends of the ages have come.**

(12) Therefore, let him who thinks he stands take heed lest he fall.

It is interesting to note that the Apostle Paul admonishes us to look to the examples of those that came before us in verse 6, and that God was not pleased because they:

Verse 6 - lusted after evil
Verse 7- they were idolaters
Verse 8- committed sexual immorality
Verse 9 - tempted the Lord
Verse 10- murmured and complained

He confirms in verse 6 that these things are examples that we should not lust after evil as they did. Verses 7-10 list those things that displeased the LORD. Verse 11 then says,

**"Now all these things happened to them as examples, and they were written for our admonition (warning), upon whom the ends of the ages have come."**

The final admonishment is profound. Verse 12 says, "Therefore let him who thinks he stands take heed lest he fall." It is very important that we know the things that please God and those things that do not please God. The Apostle Paul said that we should be careful, and these examples were written to us as a warning, and we should not make the same mistakes lest we fall. As we look at the seven hindrances to the blessing of God, it is a reminder to us that God will continually pour out his abundant blessings upon those that love him and obey his Word.

## The Blessing or Blessings?

Before we look at the seven hindrances, it is important to define the word blessing and blessings. There are some that would say that it is the blessing that is imparted upon us, and others would say the blessings. It is not my primary intention to dwell on the distinction between the two words because they literally have the same meaning.

According to *The New Strong's Exhaustive Concordance of the Bible*, the words blessing and blessings extend from the Hebrew word (1288) **bārak** which means to bless God in an act of adoration, or as a benefit to kneel, bless, congratulate, praise, or to salute. The word bless is the root word in which we get blessing or blessings. Both of these words have the same expression. The word blessing comes from the same Hebrew word (1293) **berākâ** which in *The New Strong's Exhaustive Concordance of the Bible*, means benediction or prosperity. So, in actuality they are the same words, which means to bless, or a benediction or pronunciation of prosperity.

So, in essence when God commands the blessing or blessings, it is to bless or the pronunciation of prosperity upon a people or an individual. Here are a few scriptures that show the different ways in which the LORD commanded the blessing or blessings:

Genesis 12:1-3 KJV
(1) Now the LORD had said unto Abram, Get thee out of thy country, and from thy kindred, and from thy father's house, unto a land that I will shew thee:

(2) And I will make of thee a great nation, and I will bless thee, and make thy name great; and thou shalt be a **blessing.**

(3) And I will bless them that bless thee, and curse him that curses thee: and in thee shall all families of the earth be blessed.

Genesis 27:38 KJV
(38) And Esau said unto his father, Hast thou but one **blessing**, my father? Bless me, even me also, O my father. And Esau lifted up his voice, and wept.

Genesis 49:25-26 KJV
(25) Even by the God of thy father, who shall help thee; and by the Almighty, who shall bless thee with **blessings** of heaven above, **blessings** of the deep that lie under, **blessings** of the breasts, and of the womb:
(26) The **blessings** of thy father have prevailed above the **blessings** of my progenitors unto the utmost bound of the everlasting hills: they shall be on the head of Joseph, and on the crown of the head of him that was separate from his brethren.

Deuteronomy 28:2 KJV
(2) And all these **blessings** shall come on thee, and overtake thee, if thou shalt hearken unto the voice of the LORD thy God.

Malachi 3:10 KJV
(10) Bring ye all the tithes into the storehouse, that there may be meat in mine house, and prove me now herewith, saith the LORD of hosts, if I will not open you the windows of heaven, and pour you out a **blessing**, that there shall not be room enough to receive it.

Proverbs 28:20 KJV
(20) A faithful man shall abound with **blessings,** but he that makes haste to be rich shall not be innocent.

Ephesians 1:3 KJV
(3) Blessed be the God and Father of our Lord Jesus Christ, who hath blessed us with all spiritual **blessings** in heavenly places in Christ.

# CHAPTER 2 -DISOBEDIENCE

Disobedience is defined as refusal to obey, or a failure to obey rules or someone in authority.    Sin is caused by refusal to obey or a failure to obey God's Word.  There are many scriptures and examples in the Bible that confirm that disobedience is a hindrance to the blessing of God.  Let's take a look:

"The LORD will establish you as a holy people to Himself, just as He has sworn to you, if you keep the commandments of the LORD your God and walk in His ways."
Deuteronomy 28:9 NKJV

"But it shall come to pass, if you do not obey the voice of the LORD your God, to observe carefully all His commandments and His statutes which I command you today, that all these curses will come upon you and overtake you."
Deuteronomy 28:15 NKJV

"If you are willing and obedient, you shall eat the good of the land; but if you refuse and rebel, you shall be devoured by the sword, for the mouth of the LORD has spoken."
Isaiah 1:19-20 NKJV

"Let no one deceive you with empty words, for because of these things the wrath of God comes upon the sons of disobedience."
Ephesians 5:6 NKJV

We find that the LORD is consistent throughout the Bible. From the creation of time, God has not changed. God has consistently dealt with the spirit of disobedience in the same way from the beginning of time. The Bible says that God changes not.

"Jesus Christ is the same yesterday, today, and forever."
Hebrews 13:8 NKJV

It is amazing that in the times we live today that knowledge has increased, laws have been changed, attitudes have changed but God has not changed. His attitude toward sin is the same from the beginning of time. God loves us so much and he is full of grace, mercy, kindness and compassion, but his attitude toward sin remains the same.

There are some people today that don't believe that God will judge the unrighteous, evil, and wickedness in the earth. That everyone in the end gets a free pass, and we all go to heaven, regardless of what we did while we were in the earth. This is not biblical nor is it theologically sound. Although the nature and character of God is love, patience, righteousness, and holiness, we find that God has consistently dealt with the spirit of disobedience in the same manner.
Although the LORD is much more merciful and full of grace in the New Testament, Jesus gives us a warning in Luke chapter 4.

"And Jesus answering said to him, it has been said, "You shall not tempt the Lord your God." Luke 4:12 NKJV

We find in the Word of God that disobedience caused Adam and Eve to fall short of the glory of God.

"Then to Adam He said, "Because you have heeded the voice of your wife, and have eaten from the tree of which I commanded you, saying, 'You shall not eat of it': "Cursed is the ground for your sake; in toil you shall eat of it all the days of your life."
Genesis 3:17 NKJV

Was it not disobedience that caused Moses to miss entering into the Promised Land?   Many of us know the story. In the book of Exodus, as Moses led the children of Israel through the desert to the Promised Land, they murmured and complained, and God used Moses to bring forth water miraculously by striking a rock.

Exodus 17:3-6 NKJV
(3) And the people thirsted there for water, and the people complained against Moses, and said, "Why is it you have brought us up out of Egypt, to kill us and our children and our livestock with thirst?"
(4) So, Moses cried out to the LORD, saying, "What shall I do with this people? They are almost ready to stone me!"
(5) And the LORD said to Moses, "Go on before the people, and take with you some of the elders of Israel. Also take in your hand your rod with which you struck the river, and go.
(6) Behold, I will stand before you there on the rock in Horeb; **and you shall strike the rock, and water will come out of it, that the people may drink**."
And Moses did so in the sight of the elders of Israel.

Then in the book of Numbers, we have the same account of the people murmuring and complaining about water again. This time the LORD tells Moses to speak to the rock.

Numbers 20:7-12 NKJV
(7) Then the LORD spoke to Moses, saying,
(8) "Take the rod; you and your brother Aaron gather the congregation together. **Speak to the rock before their eyes, and it will yield its water; thus, you shall bring water for them out of the rock, and give drink to the congregation and their animals**."
(9) So, Moses took the rod from before the LORD as He

commanded him.

(10) And Moses and Aaron gathered the assembly together before the rock; and he said to them, "Hear now, you rebels! Must we bring water for you out of this rock?"

(11) **Then Moses lifted his hand and struck the rock twice with his rod; and water came out abundantly, and the congregation and their animals drank.**

(12) Then the LORD spoke to Moses and Aaron, "Because you did not believe Me, to hallow Me in the eyes of the children of Israel, therefore you shall not bring this assembly into the land which I have given them."

Now let us analyze this story. In the book of Exodus, the LORD tells Moses to strike the rock to bring forth water. Moses obeys. In the book of Numbers, the LORD tells Moses to speak to the rock, and Moses strikes the rock in his anger, disobeying God. We find in verse 12 that God is not pleased with Moses' disobedience. The LORD told him to speak to the rock, but in anger he strikes the rock and God says:

"And the LORD spoke unto Moses and Aaron, because ye believed me not, to sanctify me in the eyes of the children of Israel, therefore ye shall not bring this congregation into the land which I have given them." Numbers 20:12 KJV

Isn't this interesting? Moses the man of God, who performed miracles in Egypt, parted the Red Sea, spoke with God face to face on the mountain, obtained the Ten Commandments and blueprint for the Tabernacle of Meeting was told, "You will not enter into the Promised Land because you did not sanctify me in the eyes of the children of Israel."

What was God really saying? Because you did not proclaim me, support me, obey me, do what I commanded, and deem me Holy in the eyes of Israel, you will not bring this congregation into the land in which I give to them.  Now this speaks volumes because if there is anybody who should have entered into the Promised Land it should have been Moses.  Now if God held Moses accountable, we must understand that God will also hold us accountable for obeying his Word. Disobedience hinders the blessing of God in our lives. It causes us to miss the mark and the blessing that God desires to impart to us!

Now let us look at the scriptures that deal with obedience and what the outcome is.

"Oh, that you had heeded my commandments! Then your peace would have been like a river, and your righteousness like the waves of the sea."
Isaiah 48:18 NKJV

"He who has my commandments and keeps them, it is he who loves me. And he who loves me will be loved by My Father, and I will love him and manifest myself to him."
John 14:21 NKJV

Jesus answered and said to him, "If anyone loves me, he will keep my word; and My Father will love him, and we will come to him and make our home with him.
John 14:23 NKJV

"If you keep my commandments, you will abide in my love, just as I have kept My Father's commandments and abide in His love."
 John 15:10 NKJV

Disobedience is a prevalent theme throughout the Bible, and one of the most profound examples is found in King

Saul, who was the first King of Israel in the Old Testament.

## The Israelites desire a King

The Israelites saw that the gentiles had Kings and desired to have one. They had rejected the LORD who was their King, and desired that the LORD would provide a King from among their own people, who would protect them and rule over them.

"Then all the elders of Israel gathered together and came to Samuel at Ramah, and said to him, "Look, you are old, and your sons do not walk in your ways. Now make us a king to judge us like all the nations."
1 Samuel 8:4-5 NKJV

The Lord chose Saul, a good looking handsome young man of the tribe of Benjamin.

"Now the LORD had told Samuel in his ear the day before Saul came, saying, tomorrow about this time I will send you a man from the land of Benjamin, and you shall anoint him commander over My people Israel, that he may save My people from the hand of the Philistines, for I have looked upon My people, because their cry has come to Me." So, when Samuel saw Saul, the LORD said to him, "There he is, the man of whom I spoke to you. This one shall reign over my people."
1 Samuel 9:15-17 NKJV

God answered the people's request and chose a mighty man of God amongst them by the name of Saul. There was only one thing about the man they had chosen. Although he was a handsome, good looking, humble young man, he was a disobedient man.

"Now therefore, here is the king whom you have chosen and whom you have desired. And take note, the LORD

has set a king over you. **If you fear the LORD and serve Him and obey His voice, and do not rebel against the commandment of the LORD, then both you and the king who reigns over you will continue following the LORD your God."**
"However, if you do not obey the voice of the LORD, but rebel against the commandment of the LORD, then the hand of the LORD will be against you, as it was against your fathers.  1 Samuel 12:13-15 NKJV

"It's interesting to note that although God answered their request for a King, he told them that they must still fear, serve and obey the commandments of the LORD. If they did otherwise, that the hand of the LORD would be against them.

## Kings Saul's Disobedience

   Although King Saul was the first King of Israel, his disobedience got him in trouble and caused him to lose his anointing, his favor with God, and eventually his crown.
The story begins in 1 Samuel chapter 10:8, where Samuel the Prophet anoints Saul as King and gives instructions wait seven days before offering burnt offerings and peace offerings. Samuel prophetically gave him this word because Saul would be going into battle against the Philistines. The offering of sacrifices to the LORD would be offered up unto the Lord prior to going to battle.

"Then Samuel took a flask of oil and poured it on his head, and kissed him and said: "Is it not because the LORD has anointed you commander over His inheritance?"
1 Samuel 10:1 NKJV

"You shall go down before me to Gilgal; and surely I will come down to you to offer burnt offerings and make

sacrifices of peace offerings. Seven days you shall wait, till I come to you and show you what you should do."
1 Samuel 10:8 NKJV

It concludes in 1 Samuel chapter 13 as King Saul is about to go to battle with the Philistines who have 36, 000 men prepared to fight against Israel. As the battle is preparing to kick off, fear sets in amongst God's people because of the impending battle with the Philistines' at Michmash. Circumstances seemed to be getting out of control, and Samuel the Prophet had not shown up yet to offer up burnt offerings, and peace offerings to the Lord before the battle.

"When the men of Israel saw that they were in danger (for the people were distressed), then the people hid in caves, in thickets, in rocks, in holes, and in pits. And some of the Hebrews crossed over the Jordan to the land of Gad and Gilead. As for Saul, he was still in Gilgal, and all the people followed him trembling."
1 Samuel 13:6-7 NKJV

The Bible then says that Saul waited seven days but Samuel did not show up. How many of us have gotten into trouble because we did not wait on God. Someone once said that he is an on-time God. God is never late. We may be early, and we may be late, but God is always on time. Sometimes God is even testing our patience, faith and obedience to his Word! This was Saul's test of obedience and he failed the test. Read on!

1 Samuel 13:8-14 NKJV
(8) Then he waited seven days, according to the time set by Samuel. But Samuel did not come to Gilgal; and the people were scattered from him.
(9) So, Saul said, "Bring a burnt offering and peace offerings here to me." And he offered the burnt offering.
(10) Now it happened, as soon as he had finished

presenting the burnt offering, that Samuel came; and Saul went out to meet him, that he might greet him.
(11) And Samuel said, "What have you done?" Saul said, "When I saw that the people were scattered from me, and that you did not come within the days appointed, and that the Philistines gathered together at Michmash, (12) Then I said, 'The Philistines will now come down on me at Gilgal, and I have not made supplication to the LORD.' Therefore, I felt compelled, and offered a burnt offering."
(13) And Samuel said to Saul, "You have done foolishly. You have not kept the commandment of the LORD your God, which He commanded you. For now, the LORD would have established your kingdom over Israel forever.
(14) But now your kingdom shall not continue. The LORD has sought for Himself a man after His own heart, and the LORD has commanded him to be commander over His people, because you have not kept what the LORD commanded you."

It is a travesty to hear the Prophet Samuel say in verse 13, "You have not kept the commandment of the Lord, which he commanded you." Verse 14 states: "But now your kingdom will not stand."

Child of God, what has God told you to do? What prophetic word or scripture verse has the Lord instructed you with, yet you have not obeyed? Please do not delay, know that God will hold us accountable for his Word. In the book of Luke, Jesus declared to Satan, "It is written that "man shall not live by bread alone, but by every Word of God."
Luke 4: 4 NKJV

God's word is true. Every precious promise and commandment is yes and amen. We must never, ever tempt God with our disobedience. King Saul disobeyed the Word of the LORD given by the Prophet Samuel. I can recall someone once saying that, ninety-nine and a half just won't do. We must do one hundred percent of what God tells us to do!

If we do less than what God told us to do, it is not obedience but disobedience, and it will cause us to miss the mark when we choose to do our own thing, and ignore God's Holy word. This was Saul's first act of disobedience.

Psalms 100:5 says, "The Lord is good, and his mercy endures forever." God's grace and mercy continuously gives us the ability to repent, turn around, and do the right thing. But what happens when we continue in disobedience and constantly ignore the Holy commandments of God? We must adhere to the word of God and know that God is merciful and compassionate and abounding in love, but we must understand that continued disobedience and sin will hinder the blessings of God in your life.

## King Saul continues in Disobedience

In 1 Sam 15:1-29, Saul continues in disobedience after he is given another assignment by the Lord. He is instructed to destroy Amalek, the enemy of Israel.

1 Samuel 15:1-3 NKJV
(1) Samuel also said to Saul, "The LORD sent me to anoint you king over His people, over Israel. Now therefore, heed the voice of the words of the LORD.
(2) Thus says the LORD of hosts: 'I will punish Amalek for what he did to Israel, how he ambushed him on the way when he came up from Egypt.
(3) Now go and attack Amalek, and utterly destroy all that they have, and do not spare them. But kill man and woman, infant and nursing child, ox and sheep, camel and donkey.

This sounds like a harsh commandment to follow, but God never gives us a commandment or instruction that is to hard or burdensome. (1 John 5:3)  God knew that Amalekites were evil and had to be destroyed because of what they did to Israel when they came out of Egypt.

"Then the LORD said to Moses, "Write this for a memorial in the book and recount it in the hearing of Joshua that I will utterly blot out the remembrance of Amalek from under heaven."
Exodus 17:14 NKJV
"Then he looked on Amalek, and he took up his oracle and said: "Amalek was first among the nations, but shall be last until he perishes."
Numbers 24:20 NKJV

"Therefore, it shall be, when the LORD your God has given you rest from your enemies all around, in the land which the LORD your God is giving you to possess as an inheritance, that you will blot out the remembrance of Amalek from under heaven. You shall not forget."
Deuteronomy 25:19 NKJV

When God speaks a word, it will come to pass. Every Word shall be established by the testimony of two or three witnesses. Three times, the Lord said that Amalek would be destroyed and King Saul was the chosen vessel to accomplish this.  Child of God, remember that the promises of God are yes and amen.  Whatever God has promised you or spoken through his servants the prophets, you can bet it "will come to pass."

We find in 1 Samuel 15, that the LORD gives Saul the assignment to attack and destroy Amalek, but Saul does not obey the commandment of the Lord, and instead keeps the enemy King alive and the best goods for himself and his men.  Let's read!

1 Samuel 15:7-9 NKJV
(7) And Saul attacked the Amalekites, from Havilah all the way to Shur, which is east of Egypt.
(8) He also took Agag king of the Amalekites alive, and utterly destroyed all the people with the edge of the sword.
(9) But Saul and the people spared Agag and the best of the sheep, the oxen, the fatlings, the lambs, and all that was good, and were unwilling to utterly destroy them. But everything despised and worthless, that they utterly destroyed.

What is interesting is that Saul did not complete the assignment. Not only did King Saul disobey the Lord one time, but two times and the Lord was grieved and said to Samuel:

"Now the word of the LORD came to Samuel, saying, "I greatly regret that I have set up Saul as king, for he has turned back from following me, and has not performed my commandments." And it grieved Samuel, and he cried out to the LORD all night."
1 Samuel 15:10-11 NKJV

It grieved the heart of Samuel the Prophet, that King Saul had disobeyed the Lord.
I believe that the pain Samuel felt was the heart of the Lord. It grieved Samuel because Saul had turned his back on the Lord did not do what the Lord told him to do. Child of God, hearken to the voice of the Lord and be obedient. Do not delay in obeying the commandments of the Lord. Listen to what Samuel said to the Saul:

1 Samuel 15:18-22 NKJV
(18) Now the LORD sent you on a mission, and said, 'Go, and utterly destroy the sinners, the Amalekites, and fight against them until they are consumed.'
(19) Why then did you not obey the voice of the LORD?

Why did you swoop down on the spoil, and do evil in the sight of the LORD?"
(20) And Saul said to Samuel, "But I have obeyed the voice of the LORD, and gone on the mission on which the LORD sent me, and brought back Agag king of Amalek; I have utterly destroyed the Amalekites.
(21) But the people took of the plunder, sheep and oxen, the best of the things which should have been utterly destroyed, to sacrifice to the LORD your God in Gilgal."
(22) So, Samuel said: "Has the LORD as great delight in burnt offerings and sacrifices, as in obeying the voice of the LORD? Behold, to obey is better than sacrifice, and to heed than the fat of rams.

God is Holy, righteous and without sin. When we know to do right and still sin, it is a slap in the face of God. How can we expect to receive answered prayer, or obtain a blessing from the Lord when we willfully sin against the Lord of Glory when our lives reflect a heart of disobedience toward him?

Obedience and doing the right thing is always acceptable before the LORD. Disobedience and doing the wrong thing is never acceptable before the LORD! We should always do the right thing that brings God glory, honor and praise in Jesus Name! It is important to remember that our obedience to God is not solely a matter of duty. We obey the LORD because we love Him according to John 14:23.

"Jesus answered and said to him, "If anyone loves me, he will keep my word; and my Father will love him, and we will come to him and make our home with him." John 14:23 NKJV

We must understand that the attitude of obedience is as important as the act of obedience. If we love God, we will obey Him. We may not be perfect in our obedience,

but it should be our desire is to submit to the Lord and follow after the WORD of God.
Obedience is the primary factor in receiving heavens blessings upon your life!

Saul did 99.9 percent of the job and God was not pleased. When God gives you an assignment, you must obey every commandment, and every directive of the Lord. Doing half the job is disobedience when we know the right thing to do, and willfully disobey God.  God's grace and mercy always restores the repentant heart of a sinner, but continued disobedience will lead us down a dark rebellious path that can only cause us more trouble. It is more important to be doers of the word and not just hearers.

"But be doers of the word, and not hearers only, deceiving yourselves."
James 1:22 NKJV

## Jonadab's Obedience to God: An Example to Follow

Although there are many examples of disobedience in the Bible, there are many other positive examples that were written for our learning as well.
In the book of Jeremiah chap. 35: 1-19, there is a man by the name of Jonadab the son of Rechab whose descendants were commended by the Lord for their continued obedience to their father.
Jonadab and his sons were a shining example of obedience in action that brought them praise and abundant blessings forever. The Lord told the men of Judah and the inhabitants of Jerusalem to look to their example of obedience!  Listen to the word of the Lord spoken to the Prophet Jeremiah:

Jeremiah 35:13-19 NKJV

(13) "Thus says the LORD of hosts, the God of Israel: 'Go and tell the men of Judah and the inhabitants of Jerusalem, "Will you not receive instruction to obey my words?" says the LORD.

(14) "The words of Jonadab the son of Rechab, which he commanded his sons, not to drink wine, are performed; for to this day, they drink none, and obey their father's commandment. But although I have spoken to you, rising early and speaking, you did not obey me.

(15) I have also sent to you all My servants the prophets, rising up early and sending them, saying, 'Turn now everyone from his evil way, amend your doings, and do not go after other gods to serve them; then you will dwell in the land which I have given you and your fathers.' But you have not inclined your ear, nor obeyed me.

(16) Surely the sons of Jonadab the son of Rechab have performed the commandment of their father, which he commanded them, but this people have not obeyed me." '

(17) "Therefore, thus says the LORD God of Hosts, the God of Israel: 'Behold, I will bring on Judah and on all the inhabitants of Jerusalem all the doom that I have pronounced against them; because I have spoken to them but they have not heard, and I have called to them but they have not answered.' "

(18) And Jeremiah said to the house of the Rechabites, "Thus says the LORD of hosts, the God of Israel: 'Because you have obeyed the commandment of Jonadab your father, and kept all his precepts and done according to all that he commanded you,

(19) therefore, thus says the LORD of hosts, the God of Israel: "Jonadab the son of Rechab shall not lack a man to stand before Me forever."

Obedience brings abundant blessings, but continued and willful disobedience brings swift judgment in Jesus' name!

## The Parable of the Two Sons

Jesus told the parable of two sons, one was obedient, the other disobedient. Jesus said that the one that obeyed his Father did what was asked of him, the other did not.

Matthew 21:28-31 NKJV
(28) "But what do you think? A man had two sons, and he came to the first and said, 'Son, go work today in my vineyard.'
(29) He answered and said, 'I will not,' but afterward he regretted it and went.
(30) Then he came to the second and said likewise. And he answered and said, 'I go, sir,' but he did not go.
(31) Which of the two did the will of his father?" They said to Him, "The first." Jesus said to them, "Assuredly, I say to you that tax collectors and harlots enter the kingdom of God before you.

This is an interesting parable told by the Lord. A man had two sons and he asked the first one to go work in his vineyard.  The first son says no, but later repents and went. He asks the second son to go work in the vineyard and he says yes, but he did not go.
Jesus then asks the question, "Which of the two did the will of his father?" The religious leaders answer correctly that the first son did.  Jesus then says in verse 31, "I say to you that the tax collectors and harlots enter the kingdom of God before you."

This is an amazing parable, because Jesus is saying there are some who say, "I go sir, but do not go." Then there are others who say I will not go, but do go." There is some revelation in this parable. There are two sons, one is obedient, and the other is disobedient. This is an interesting parable, because Jesus told the religious leaders that they are disobedient. They are the ones who say, I go sir, but do not go. The obedient ones are the sinners who say I will not go, but repent and do go. The one who responds in obedience does the will of the father and enters into the Kingdom of God.

Solomon, the wise man in the Bible said:
Ecclesiastes 12:13-14 KJV
13  Let us hear the conclusion of the whole matter: Fear God, and keep his commandments: for this is the whole duty of man.
14  For God shall bring every work into judgment, with every secret thing, whether it be good, or whether it be evil.

## Peter and Apostles Obey God

In the book of Acts chapter 5: 16-29, there is an interesting story of Peter and the Apostles preaching the Gospel, healing the sick, and casting out unclean spirits. The high priest and the Sadducees were filled with anger and had them locked up.  They were thrown in jail, but an angel of the Lord opened the prison doors and brought them out.

The Angel of the Lord then proclaimed, "Go! Stand and speak all the words of this Life to the people in the temple." They immediately went back to the temple proclaiming the Gospel to the people again obeying God.

Listen to the account:
Acts 5:25-29 NKJV
(25) So, one came and told them, saying, "Look, the men whom you put in prison are standing in the temple and teaching the people!"
(26) Then the captain went with the officers and brought them without violence, for they feared the people, lest they should be stoned.
(27) And when they had brought them, they set them before the council. And the high priest asked them,

(28) saying, "Did we not strictly command you not to teach in this name? And look, you have filled Jerusalem with your doctrine, and intend to bring this Man's blood on us!"

**(29) But Peter and the other apostles answered and said: "We ought to obey God rather than men.**

The Apostles then said something profound:

Acts 5:30-32 NKJV

(30) The God of our fathers raised up Jesus whom you murdered by hanging on a tree.

(31) Him God has exalted to His right hand to be Prince and Savior, to give repentance to Israel and forgiveness of sins.

(32) **And we are His witnesses to these things, and so also is the Holy Spirit whom God has given to those who obey Him."**

We must remember that it is better to obey God than to obey man. In fact, it is better to obey God period! When we obey God, there is no need to worry. God will protect you. David said in Psalm 27: 1, "The LORD is my light and my salvation, whom shall I fear? The LORD is the strength of my life, of whom shall I be afraid?"

Child of God, there is no need to be afraid when we are walking with God, he will protect you and shield you. Peter and the Apostles knew this, and they proudly proclaimed, **"We ought to obey God rather than men."** This is a word of wisdom to all believers, and it is a profound word indeed. God's blessing shall encamp about the obedient servant and believer. When we trust God and stand on his precious promises and Holy commandments he will protect us from all hurt, harm and danger.

"Do you not know that to whom you present yourselves slaves to obey, you are that one's slaves whom you obey,

whether of sin leading to death, or of obedience leading to righteousness?"
Romans 6:16 NKJV

There are five things we must remember about obedience!
1. The prerequisite for God's best provision and blessings is obedience and faith. This is found throughout the Bible in scripture.
2. Radical obedience is what God is looking for in the believer.
3. The core root of all sin is disobedience to God's established authority.
4. True obedience is hearing the Word of God, applying it your heart, and walking in it.
This is where you get your blessing!
5. Whenever we disobey what God has clearly revealed to us, we bring ourselves under the influence of rebellion, and the Bible states that rebellion is as the sin of witchcraft.

Jesus said in John 14:21-24 NKJV
(21) He who has My commandments and keeps them, it is he who loves Me. And he who loves Me will be loved by My Father, and I will love him and manifest Myself to him."
(22) Judas (not Iscariot) said to Him, "Lord, how is it that You will manifest Yourself to us, and not to the world?"
(23) Jesus answered and said to him, "If anyone loves Me, he will keep My word; and My Father will love him, and We will come to him and make Our home with him.
(24) He who does not love me does not keep my words; and the word which you hear is
not mine but the Fathers who sent me.

How can we expect to have a fruitful relationship with the LORD, when our lives do not reflect a heart of obedience to him. We must remember that disobedience leads to rebellion, and rebellion is as the sin of witchcraft. (1 Sam 15: 23)

"O foolish Galatians! Who has bewitched you that you should not obey the truth, before whose eyes Jesus Christ was clearly portrayed among you as crucified?" Galatians 3:1 NKJV

## The Greatest Example of Obedience - Jesus Christ

One of the greatest examples of obedience in scripture is of the Lord Jesus Christ. His example of obedience is exemplified through his suffering and death at the cross, and is mentioned in Hebrews 5: 7-8.

(Heb 5:7) For Jesus, in the days of His flesh, when He had offered up prayers and supplications with strong crying's and tears to Him who was able to save Him from death, and was heard in that He feared,
(Heb 5:8) **though being a Son, yet He learned obedience by the things which He suffered.**
(Heb 5:9) And being perfected, **He became the Author of eternal salvation to all those who obey Him**.

Even in the face of great pain and intense suffering, more than he could bear. Jesus chose obedience, though it meant severe hardship and death at the cross. Yet his obedience was the ultimate act of selfless sacrifice that saved all that believe on his name! This is the ultimate example of obedience to the Father, and is an example for all of us to follow.

Isaiah 1:18-19 NKJV
(18) "Come now, and let us reason together," Says the LORD, "Though your sins are like scarlet, They shall be

as white as snow; Though they are red like crimson, They shall be as wool.
(19) If you are willing and obedient, You shall eat the good of the land;

Willingness and obedience go hand in hand. It is the attitude which makes the difference. Obedience deals with our responsive actions toward authority. Submission deals with our attitude toward authority. This is where many of us miss it.

God looks at our outward actions and the hidden attitude of our hearts. Good intentions will not stand the judgement of God. Only true faith, which is evidenced by corresponding works of obedience, will stand. Mark Rutland in his book, *Nevertheless,* told the story of a great missionary by the name of C.T. Studd who set the example of obedience when he was in his fifties. While laboring for the Lord, he was sick and burdened with an invalid wife in India for many years preaching the Gospel.

When leaving India for England for a well-deserved rest, he heard the voice of God direct him to Central Africa. According to Rutland, "In the nineteenth century, Central Africa was considered a "missionary's graveyard."
It would seem selfish and ungodly to leave his wife to go to a place such as this. He didn't even have support from a missionary board. He was criticized, and his missionary trip was highly controversial. Yet he obeyed God and was used mightily of God. As a result, revival came to Africa!

There are many examples in the Bible of those who were obedient to the Lord. Moses was given instructions to go before Pharoah, one of the mightiest men of that time. He obeyed God, and mighty miracles and a great deliverance for the children of Israel came as a result of his obedience to the Word of God!

Jesus set the perfect example for all believers. If we suffer for the cause of Christ, we must realize that it is not in vain. The book of Philippians gives us a profound example of Jesus Christ's obedience and the result of it.

Philippians 2:5-11 NKJV
(5) Let this mind be in you which was also in Christ Jesus,
(6) who, being in the form of God, did not consider it robbery to be equal with God,
(7) but made Himself of no reputation, taking the form of a bondservant, and coming in the likeness of men.
**(8) And being found in appearance as a man, He humbled Himself and became obedient to the point of death, even the death of the cross.**
(9) Therefore, God also has highly exalted Him and given Him the name which is above every name,
(10) that at the name of Jesus every knee should bow, of those in heaven, and of those on earth, and of those under the earth,
(11) and that every tongue should confess that Jesus Christ is Lord, to the glory of God the Father.

Notice in Phil 2: 8-9, that the exaltation came after the obedience. In the beginning of the chapter, we talked about Adams disobedience that brought sin to mankind. When we contrast this with Christ's obedience and death at the cross, eternal life was granted to every human being that believes on his name.

"For as by one man's disobedience many were made sinners, so by the obedience of one shall many be made righteous." Romans 5:19 NKJV

Although the grace of God sustains us, true obedience to the Word of God will cause an overflow of grace and blessings to be released in our lives. We must always follow the example of Jesus Christ, who is the ultimate example of obedience!

# CHAPTER 3 - IDOLATRY

Someone may be asking the question, "Why is it so important that we know about hindrances to the blessings of God?" First of all, let us take a lot at a profound scripture that Jesus gave us in John 10:10.

"The thief cometh not, but for to steal, and to kill, and to destroy: I am come that they might have life, and that they might have it more abundantly." John 10:10 KJV

So, we find throughout the bible that it is Gods' desire is to bless his people with life more abundantly. Yet, the thief desires to kill, steal and to destroy. The biggest thief that I know of in scripture is Satan. Isn't he the one that desires to keep us from fulfilling purpose and destiny? Isn't he the one that attempted to hinder Adam and Eve in the garden by hindering the blessing of God on their lives through disobedience? Isn't he the one that has attempted to steal true worship from the one true God, Jehovah, and caused men and women to miss the mark since the Garden of Eden?

The Apostle Paul said, "Lest Satan should get an advantage of us, we are not ignorant of his devices." (2 Cor 2:11) There are many devices that he uses against us, but one of the primary devices we find in scripture is idolatry! All throughout Old Testament history we find the sin of idolatry caused God's people to fall short of God's glory, and hindered the blessing of God when they engaged in idolatrous behavior. Many of us are familiar with the golden calf of Exodus chapter 32. The people were indulging in idolatrous behavior while Moses was on the mountain with God.

Idolatry in the Bible is the opposite of true worship to the Most High God. It is recorded throughout scripture and caused many men and women to miss the mark, and hindered them from having a blessed relationship with the Lord. God in his infinite love will always bestow his wondrous grace and mercy upon us, because his mercies are new every morning. Yet, we must be obedient to worship him in the beauty of his Holiness. (Psalm 96: 9) Idolatry in any form is sin. It is a spiritual hindrance that blocks Gods' blessings upon our lives. As it relates to our relationship with the LORD, idolatry obstructs, impedes, and hinders the blessing of God in our lives.

So, what is idolatry? Webster's defines idolatry as the worship of idols or images. It is also the extreme admiration, love or reverence for something or someone. Idolatry can be defined in two ways:

1. The worship of images, statues, pictures, things made by hands, or the worship of the heavenly bodies, which are the sun, moon, and stars, it is also false gods, demons, angels, humans and or animals.

2. The excessive attachment or veneration for anything, or that which borders on adoration. In other words, it is anything that is at the root of a person's worship, something that you apply your energy, your heart and love too.

It can also be anything that you cling to, hold on to, exalt and allow to take the place of the one true God. Anything that we put our time and energy in, and exalt above God can become an idol. Although we may not worship idols as they did in the past, there are many things in the world today that can become an idol such as the world, money, power and even sex.

Relationships can be idols as well, such as exalting a man or woman above God. Anything that becomes a false dependency, and becomes the focus of our attention can be defined as an idol as well. Jesus said in Matthew

6:21, "For where your treasure is, there your heart will be also." One of the primary causes of idolatry is the heart condition. If the soil of your heart is good ground for the Word, and you receive it with joy, you will reap the benefits and produce good fruit.

"But other fell into good ground, and brought forth fruit, some a hundredfold, some sixtyfold, some thirtyfold." Matthew 13:8 KJV

If the soil of your heart is shallow or stony, there is no way that the seed of the Word, when sown will take root to grow and produce good fruit.

"And when he sowed, some seeds fell by the way side, and the fowls came and devoured them up: Some fell upon stony places, where they had not much earth: and forthwith they sprung up, because they had no deepness of earth: And when the sun was up, they were scorched; and because they had no root, they withered away." (Matthew 13:4-6 KJV)

If you lack a heart that is obedient and hot toward the Lord, and you are lukewarm in your relationship with the Lord, it will be easy for Satan to enter in and draw you away.
I have a question? What is it in your life today that has stolen your affections from God? What is it in your life that is hindering your spiritual growth? Is it money, is your job, or is it something that steals your time from God? Is it something in your life that is perceived way more important than prayer, the study of the Word, or attending church?

We must be careful because when we think of idols, what comes to mind is what we read in the scriptures, and most of the idols in scripture are of stone or wood. Yet, the truth of the matter is that an idol is anything that steals your affections from the Lord. When you begin to idolize or put something or someone on a platform higher than God, and allow it to replace God, it becomes idolatry, and idolatry is sin.

Many people put their heart and soul into things that have replaced true worship to the LORD. It has become a symbol of idolatry. If you have no time for studying the Word, something has replaced that. If you have no time for prayer, something has replaced that. If you have no time to attend worship service, something has replaced that. We need to understand that God is our source, everything else is a resource. It is amazing that we give so many things' 100% percent of our time and energy. Yet, when it comes to God, we say God understands. Then we never spend time with him, or tell him how much we love him and appreciate him. What kind of relationship is that?

Do you want to be in a relationship with someone who never communicates with you, never spends time with you, or never says I love you, or appreciates you? This is how many believers are in their relationship with the LORD. This is how many of us treat the lover of our souls. But yet, we want blessings of God, and we want God to move heaven and earth on our behalf when we are in dire straits!

We have young people that have become attached to video games, and unknowingly, it has become an idol. There are people that idolize rock stars, rap stars, athletes, movie stars, and even money. It has become an idol.

Deep down within every person is the desire to worship, adore, exalt, and praise the creator. If it is not focused on the one who created us and fashioned us in his image, it becomes an idol. Satan has truly deceived the masses, and we even find that many believers have been deceived as well. When our focus is taken off of what God commanded in his Holy Word, it is possible to be deceived into doing exactly what the enemy wants, which is to focus on the things of this world, and the cares of this world rather than the Creator of the world!

We must be careful, because the very thing that God provides to bless us can become a snare to us. God gives us money, but we should not love money, less it become a snare and an idol, and separate us from us from God. God gives us jobs, but jobs shouldn't steal our time and energy and become our source. Jobs are a resource and not our source. God gives us education, but education is to inform and expand our knowledge. It shouldn't become the focal point of our knowledge. Only God can give us true wisdom, knowledge and understanding.

We must be careful because (television) tell-lie-vision opens the door to idolatry if we are not careful. We often find young people imitating what they see on television. American author Og Mandino wrote, "Never imitate another, for how do you that you may not imitate evil. "And he who imitates evil always goes beyond the example set.
While he who imitates what is good always falls short. Imitate nothing or no one. Be yourself." People of God we must look to Christ who is the Savior of the world and the ultimate example to follow. Today many people have sold their soul to the devil for riches and fame. In the book of Exodus, the LORD gave the people of God a very strict command:

Exodus 20:1-6 KJV
(1) And God spoke all these words, saying,
(2) I am the LORD thy God, which have brought thee out of the land of Egypt, out of the house of bondage.
(3) Thou shalt have no other gods before me.

(4)  Thou shalt not make unto thee any graven image, or any likeness of anything that is in heaven above, or that is in the earth beneath, or that is in the water under the earth:

(5)  Thou shalt not bow down thyself to them, nor serve them: for I the LORD thy God
am a jealous God, visiting the iniquity of the fathers upon the children unto the third and fourth generation of them that hate me;

(6)  And shewing mercy unto thousands of them that love me, and keep my commandments.

When we look at Exodus 20 we find something interesting. God gives a commandment that we should have no other gods before him. (notice the little "g") We should not even make images or any likeness of anything in the heavens, earth or water. God said we should not bow down to them or to serve them! In other words, the LORD was saying, **"I am the One True God, I am the only one worthy of worship!"**

"And the LORD shall be King over all the earth. In that day it shall be "The LORD is one," And His name one." Zechariah 14:9 NKJV

The LORD even states that if we do bow down to these idols, that he would judge that person even unto the third and fourth generations. (Verse 5)  Now contrast that with verse 6 that states, he will show mercy to thousands that love him, and keep his commandments. Did you get that?  In other words, idolatry is a hindrance and a curse, but when we love God; mercy, grace and blessings are imparted unto us!

We find that the Israelites had a history of worshipping idols.  In the book of Numbers chapter 2 something interesting happened as they journeyed to the Promised Land.  Let's take a look!  While journeying to the Promised Land, the people of God began to murmur and complain against Moses and the LORD because of the difficult journey. Listen to the Biblical account:

"Then they journeyed from Mount Hor by the Way of the Red Sea, to go around the land of Edom; and the soul of the people became very discouraged on the way. And the people spoke against God and against Moses: "Why have you brought us up out of Egypt to die in the wilderness? For there is no food and no water, and our soul loathes this worthless bread." Numbers 21:4-5 NKJV

As the people of God journeyed to the Promised Land under the leadership of Moses, they got discouraged. As a result, they began to murmur and complain against God and Moses. As a result, God sent fiery serpents among them!

"So, the LORD sent fiery serpents among the people, and they bit the people, and many of the people of Israel died. " Numbers 21:6 NKJV

How many of us know that there is some revelation in this. No matter how tough the journey of life gets, we should be thankful to the Lord for his grace and mercy. Yet sometimes we do the same thing as the Israelites. We get discouraged and upset, we murmur and complain, and God, in his infinite wisdom has to show us that he is God! One thing I have found is that the LORD will discipline us in the way that he desires. He can even use the devil as an instrument of discipline!

"So, the people came to Moses and said, "We have sinned, because we have spoken against the Lord and you. Intercede with the Lord, that He may remove the serpents from us." "And Moses interceded for the people." Numbers 21: 7 NKJV
What happens next is strange, and I'm sure none of us really understand it, but God did something very interesting in which we will explain later.

"Then the LORD said to Moses, "Make a fiery serpent, and set it on a pole; and it shall be that everyone who is bitten, when he looks at it, shall live." Numbers 21:8 NKJV

Let's be truthful for a moment. Isn't this a strange thing that God asked Moses to do? But there is some revelation in it that points to Jesus Christ. Just for a moment let's think about this. God does everything for a reason!

He asked Noah to build a large ark to prepare for rain that would house hundreds of animals. He sent a little shepherd boy named David to fight against a giant skilled warrior named Goliath, who was about nine to eleven feet tall. He gave Moses a blueprint to construct a place of worship called the Tabernacle in the wilderness with different colors, animal skins and medals, which the natural person cannot understand. He told a Syrian General named Naaman to dip seven times in some dirty water and he would be healed of leprosy. Yes, my friend, God asks us to do some strange things at times, but it is all for his glory!

Let's get back to our story! As the Israelites journeyed toward the Promised Land, they murmured and complained, and the LORD sent fiery serpents to discipline them. As the serpent's bit them, they pleaded with Moses to intercede for them before the Lord to remove the serpents!

That apparently did not happen, but the LORD, being rich in mercy and compassion, responded to the merciful pleas of his people in a rather unexpected fashion. The scripture says God gave Moses some rather unique instructions. The LORD told Moses to construct a pole with a bronze serpent on it, and if someone was bitten by the serpents, they could look at the bronze serpent on the pole and live!

Now some of us know the story, others are saying, "What in the world did God do that for?" Remember I said that God does everything for a reason!

"So, Moses made a bronze serpent, and put it on a pole; and so it was, if a serpent had bitten anyone, when he looked at the bronze serpent, he lived." (Numbers 21:9 NKJV)

The Lord provided an interesting means of healing, whereby those bitten could survive the serpent bites by looking at the bronze serpent on a pole and they would live!

What is interesting is that we still have this symbol today in the medical profession; which is a symbol that represents medical help to those that need it. Does this look familiar? (see diagram)

**(Diagram)**

This symbol is one that is used in the medical field. We see it on ambulances and hospital personnel that come to render medical aid to us. The world has taken this symbol from the Bible and it represents medical health or healing.

This instrument of healing was first used by God, and given by Moses to the people to heal them from serpent bites.
What is interesting is that after many years it became an idol to the Israelites! Later on, in the history of the Israelites we find that King Hezekiah was still dealing with this instrument of healing that was given to Moses many years earlier.

2 Kings 18:1-4 NKJV
(1) Now it came to pass in the third year of Hoshea the son of Elah, king of Israel, that Hezekiah the son of Ahaz, king of Judah, began to reign.
(2) He was twenty-five years old when he became king, and he reigned twenty-nine years in Jerusalem. His mother's name was Abi the daughter of Zechariah.
(3) And he did what was right in the sight of the LORD,

according to all that his father David had done.
**(4) He removed the high places and broke the sacred pillars, cut down the wooden image and broke in pieces the bronze serpent that Moses had made. For until those days the children of Israel burned incense to it, and called it Nehushtan.**

The Bible says that during the reforms of King Hezekiah, "He removed the high places and broke in pieces the bronze serpent that Moses had made, for until those days the sons of Israel burned incense to it, and it was called Nehushtan" (2 Kings 18:4).

When we read verses 5-7, we find that Hezekiah did not practice idolatry. It was not a hindrance or snare to him, and as a result God blessed him!

2 Kings 18:5-7 KJV
(5) He trusted in the LORD God of Israel; so that after him was none like him among all the kings of Judah, nor any that were before him.
(6) For he clave to the LORD, and departed not from following him, **but kept his commandments, which the LORD commanded Moses.**
(7) **And the LORD was with him; and he prospered whithersoever he went forth**: and he rebelled against the king of Assyria, and served him not.

Did you get that? He did not allow idolatry to hinder him and he kept the word of God, and God blessed and prospered him! As we stated earlier, idolatry is a snare and a hindrance to the blessings of God. Nevertheless, those that follow after his Word will reap the blessings of heaven! Now think with me for a moment. Isn't it amazing that after all those years that the people of God still had that bronze serpent on a pole, and people were burning incense to it for worship? Let's take a look at this. From Numbers, Deuteronomy, Joshua, Judges, Ruth, 1 Samuel, 2 Samuel, 1 Kings and then 2 Kings! Good God from Zion! You mean to tell me that all those years that someone still had that bronze serpent and was still burning incense to it as an idol?

Isn't it the same today? People today have made idols of symbols, emblems and rituals. We find that the Israelites gave undue significance to a material object that no longer had any power. I believe that many people do the same thing today. They read horoscopes, they have lucky charms, rabbit's foot, four leaf clovers, and the list goes on.

Isn't it interesting that the emblem the LORD chose for the Israelites in the wilderness was a serpent? Most people find serpents to be repelling and repulsive, but God used it as a symbol of life! Here is the wisdom in this!

The people of Israel had a choice to make. They could die from the bite of the serpents, or they could look to the bronze serpent and live. Those who did not want to look upon it, or refused to look upon it, died.

Today, we have a choice. There have been many people bitten by the serpent of old, who is Satan, and through sin, they have died or may be dying spiritually in the wilderness of this world. But just as the Israelites looked to the bronze serpent on the pole, we can now look to Jesus' death at the cross, fix our eyes upon him, and in simple trusting faith, we can believe in our heart, and confess with our mouth that Jesus is Lord, be saved, and have life eternal life!

Romans 10:9-11 KJV
(9) That if you shalt confess with your mouth the Lord Jesus, and shall believe in your heart that God hath raised him from the dead, you shalt be saved.
(10) For with the heart man believes unto righteousness;

and with the mouth confession is made unto salvation. (11) For the scripture saith, whosoever believes on him shall not be ashamed.

What is interesting is that the symbol of the cross, which was a Roman instrument of death, became the symbol of life! Praise God!

Just as it was with the Israelites, God did not remove the serpent from the wilderness but used it as an instrument of his own will. Today the LORD has not removed Satan from the world. There is an appointed time that this will happen. The devil is still in the world deceiving and biting people every day. His deadly venom is everywhere, but God has provided a remedy, which is visible for all to see; JESUS CHRIST!

The book of Hebrews says:
"Looking unto Jesus, the author and finisher of our faith, who for the joy that was set before Him endured the cross, despising the shame, and has sat down at the right hand of the throne of God."
Hebrews 12:2 NKJV

Many people may not be familiar with the serpent in the wilderness scripture, but they are familiar with John 3: 14-16:

"And as Moses lifted up the serpent in the wilderness, even so must the Son of Man be lifted up, that whoever believes in Him should not perish but have eternal life. "For God so loved the world that He gave His only begotten Son, that whoever believes in Him should not perish but have everlasting life."
John 3:14-16 NKJV

Jesus became a curse for us that we might live. Through Jesus Christ sacrifice, the curse became the cure. By the sovereign grace of God, the curse became the very basis for our salvation! Let's take a look:

1.  Even as the serpent was lifted up on the pole, so Jesus Christ was lifted up on the cross.
2.  Even as the Israelites looked at the bronze serpent for healing, so sinners must look to Christ for salvation.
3.  The only way the Israelites could be healed was by faith. They had to look at the bronze serpent on the pole.
4.  Even though it seems ridiculous to many people. The only way that one can receive salvation is by faith in the blood of Jesus Christ through his death at the cross.
5.  Just as the Israelites looked at the bronze serpent and were healed, so can every person that looks to the cross, and believes on the Lord Jesus Christ be healed, delivered and set free!

Someone needs to know today, that whatever appears to be bad, God is turning around for your good. That which you thought was going to hurt you, God is going to use to bless you. That which appears to be a curse, will become your blessing!
That which you thought was going to kill you is going to give you life!

Someone needs to know today that all things are working together for good, to them
that love God, and are called according to his purpose. (Romans 8: 28)
The only prerequisite is to have faith in Jesus Christ, and to accept him as Lord and Savior. We must worship him alone, and cast away all worthless idols that will hinder our relationship with the Lord. We must always remember the words of Jesus Christ in the wilderness when we told Satan:

"And Jesus answered and said unto him, Get thee behind me, Satan: for it is written, Thou shalt worship the Lord thy God, and him only shalt thou serve. "Luke 4:8 KJV

You see, God desires true worship. Jesus said it plain and simple. We must worship the LORD our God, and him only we shall serve!  Idolatry hinders the blessing of God in our lives. The Apostle Paul mentions idolatry as one of the things that hinders us from inheriting the Kingdom of God!

Galatians 5:19-21 (KJV)
(19)  Now the works of the flesh are manifest, which are these; Adultery, fornication, uncleanness, lasciviousness,
(20)  **Idolatry,** witchcraft, hatred, variance, emulations, wrath, strife, seditions, heresies,
(21)  Envyings, murders, drunkenness, reveling, and such like: of which I tell you before, as I have also told you in time past, that they which do such things shall not inherit the kingdom of God.

Isn't it interesting that idolatry is mentioned among the works of the flesh! Paul even states that you cannot inherit the Kingdom of God when you practice idolatry or witchcraft. I would add sorcery and divination to this list, because they are all connected and come from the same source. It was never God's intention that the work of human hands, or that which the Lord created would become an object of affection or devotion. Idolatry is a hindrance and a snare when we take our eyes off Jesus Christ, who is King of Kings and LORD of Lords.  Our devotion and true worship must always be to the Lord and to him alone!

**SCRIPTURES ON TRUE WORSHIP**

Psalms 29:2 KJV
(2)  Give unto the LORD the glory due unto his name; worship the LORD in the beauty of holiness.

Psalms 96:9 KJV
(9)  O worship the LORD in the beauty of holiness: fear

before him, all the earth.

Matthew 4:10 NKJV
(10) Then Jesus said to him, Go, Satan! For it is written,
"You shall worship the Lord your God, and Him only you
shall serve."

John 4:23-24 KJV
(23) But the hour comes, and now is, when the true
worshippers shall worship the Father in spirit and in
truth: for the Father seeks such to worship him.
(24) God is a Spirit: and they that worship him must
worship him in spirit and in truth.

Revelation 14:7 KJV
(7) Saying with a loud voice, Fear God, and give glory to
him; for the hour of his judgment is come: and worship
him that made heaven, and earth, and the sea, and the
fountains of waters.

Revelation 22:8-9 KJV
(8) And I John saw these things, and heard them, and
when I had heard and seen, I fell down to worship before
the feet of the angel which shewed me these things.
(9) Then saith he unto me, See thou do it not: for I am
thy fellow servant, and of thy brethren the prophets and
of them which keep the sayings of this book: worship
God.

# CHAPTER 4 - PRIDE

Pride is one word that is the root and destruction of many in the world and the body of Christ. Isn't it interesting to note that in the word Pride, the letter "I" is in the center of the word. You can tell when someone is walking in the spirit of pride because they have to be the center of attention. The focus is on them and about them, and they lift themselves above everyone else. Before we move into the third hindrance to the blessings of God, let's define pride.

Pride is defined as inordinate self-esteem. An unreasonable conceit of one's own superiority in talents, beauty, accomplishments, rank or elevation in office, which manifests itself in lofty airs, distance, reserve, and often in contempt of others. In other words, it means to value one's self above all others.

"Everyone proud in heart is an abomination to the LORD; though they join forces, none will go unpunished."
Proverbs 16:5 NKJV

"Pride goes before destruction and a haughty spirit before a fall. Better to be of a humble spirit with the lowly, than to divide the spoil with the proud."
Proverbs 16:18-19 NKJV

From the beginning of time, God made man and woman in his image to fellowship and worship him. God never intended for man to exalt himself above others, to walk in arrogance or to be high-minded. God created us to humbly worship and exalt him.
So, the question is? Where did this haughtiness, pride and self-exaltation come from? The Bible gives us a clue. From the beginning of time there was one who walked with God, who covered the throne of God, and who

worshipped God. But he decided in his heart that he wanted to be God.

He decided that he wanted to be exalted above the Most High God. That very being who I am speaking of is none other than the evil one, Satan, Lucifer, the adversary, the devil, the prince of darkness and the chief of the fallen angels.

## The Prophet Isaiah speaks of Satan's Pride

The Prophet Isaiah describes Lucifer's fall in Isaiah 14:12-17 NKJV
(12) "How you are fallen from heaven, O Lucifer, son of the morning! How you are cut down to the ground, you who weakened the nations!
(13) For you have said in your heart: 'I will ascend into heaven, I will exalt my throne above the stars of God; I will also sit on the mount of the congregation on the farthest sides of the north;
(14) I will ascend above the heights of the clouds. I will be like the Most High.'
(15) Yet you shall be brought down to Sheol, to the lowest depths of the Pit.
(16) "Those who see you will gaze at you, and consider you, saying: 'Is this the man who made the earth tremble, who shook kingdoms,
(17) Who made the world as a wilderness and destroyed its cities, who did not open the house of his prisoners?'

Notice in verse 13, it says, "For you have said in your heart" Pride always begins in the heart.

"A good man out of the good treasure of his heart brings forth good; and an evil man out of the evil treasure of his heart brings forth evil. For out of the abundance of the heart his mouth speaks."
Luke 6:45 NKJV

Sometime long ago, according to scripture Satan's dwelling place was in Heaven. His name was Lucifer. He dwelt there with the Most High God and covered the throne of God. History records that he was a wonderful musician who made melodies in heaven, but he attempted to exalt himself upon the throne of God in pride and rebellion and was cast out of heaven, taking with him a third of the angels.

"So, the great dragon was cast out, that serpent of old, called the Devil and Satan, who deceives the whole world; he was cast to the earth, and his angels were cast out with him." Revelation 12:9 NKJV

Verse 12 states, ""How you are fallen from heaven, O Lucifer, son of the morning! How you are cut down to the ground, you who weakened the nations!"

Satan would be what I call an "I - specialist." An "I-specialist is prideful, haughty, arrogant, high minded, and self-exalted. Isaiah records that he said in his heart, "I will go up to the heavens, I will exalt my throne above the stars of God, I will also sit on the mount of the congregation, in the sides of the north."

The north is symbolic of Gods throne, it is His place of dwelling in heaven. Satan goes on to say, "I will go up above the heights of the clouds; I will be like the Most High." (Verse 14) Anytime a person begins to lift himself up, watch out. Someone said that pride is like bad breath. They are always the last one to smell it, when everybody else already has.

The Bible records in Proverbs 6: 17, that God hates a proud look. I believe that this verse alone says it all. God hates a proud look. Why does he hate it? Because he knows what pride can do to a person. He knows that it can lead to destructive behavior, division and dissension wherever it is manifested. What was Gods response to Satan's pride?

In verse 14; God says, "Yet you will be brought down to hell, to the sides of the pit."
Jesus records in Luke 10: 18 that he witnessed it all. Satan was indeed brought to hell.

"And He said to them, "I saw Satan fall like lightning from heaven."
Luke 10:18 NKJV

Jesus said in Luke 14:11, "That whoever exalts himself shall be abased, and he who humbles himself shall be exalted," In other words, if you humble yourself, God will lift you up. If you exalt yourself, you will be brought down. The word abased in Webster's 1828 dictionary defines abased as reduced to a low state, humbled, or degraded.

This is exactly what happened to Satan. God abased him. He cast him down to hell. He was reduced to a low state and degraded. Isaiah 14:16 confirms it and said, "Those who see you shall stare and closely watch you, saying, Is this the man who made the earth to tremble; who shook kingdoms?" Anytime you walk in the spirit of pride, there is only one way to go and that is down.

## The Prophet Ezekiel speaks of Satan's Pride

In the book of Ezekiel chap 28, Ezekial describes in detail the ruler of Tyre in whom the Lord God Almighty pronounced judgment. Many scholars would agree that this pronounced judgment is identical to Isaiah's description of Lucifer who attempted to exalt himself above the throne of God.

Ezekiel 28:11-19 NKJV

(11) Moreover, the word of the LORD came to me, saying,

(12) "Son of man, take up a lamentation for the king of Tyre, and say to him, 'Thus says the Lord GOD: "You were the seal of perfection, Full of wisdom and perfect in beauty.

(13) You were in Eden, the garden of God; every precious stone was your covering: The Sardius, Topaz, and Diamond, Beryl, Onyx, Jasper, Sapphire, Turquoise, and Emerald with gold. The workmanship of your timbrels and pipes was prepared for you on the day you were created.

(14) "You were the anointed cherub who covers. I established you; you were on the holy mountain of God; you walked back and forth in the midst of fiery stones.

(15) You were perfect in your ways from the day you were created, till iniquity was found in you.

(16) "By the abundance of your trading you became filled with violence within, and you sinned; therefore, I cast you as a profane thing Out of the mountain of God; And I destroyed you, O covering cherub, From the midst of the fiery stones.

(17) "Your heart was lifted up because of your beauty; you corrupted your wisdom for the sake of your splendor; I cast you to the ground, I laid you before kings, That they might gaze at you.

(18) "You defiled your sanctuaries by the multitude of your iniquities, by the iniquity of your trading; therefore, I brought fire from your midst; It devoured you, And I turned you to ashes upon the earth In the sight of all who saw you.

(19) All who knew you among the peoples are astonished at you; you have become a horror, and shall be no more forever."


Ezekiel describes in detail the judgement against the Prince of Tyre and his nation, but there are many allegorical references to Satan who lifted himself up and was cast down. Ezekiel 28:13-14 describes in detail that he was in Eden, the garden of God.

When we read the Genesis account of the fall of Adam and Eve in the Garden of Eden, Satan was the only other individual who was in the garden other than Adam and Eve!

The Bible also says that he was musically inclined. Verse 13 says, "The workmanship of your tambourines and of your flutes was prepared in you in the day that you were created."

The Bible also says that before he was judged and cursed, he covered the throne of God. Verse 14 states, "You were the anointed cherub who covers. I established you; You were on the holy mountain of God; You walked back and forth in the midst of fiery stones." Verse 17 pronounced the judgment; "Your heart was lifted up because of your beauty. You have spoiled your wisdom because of your brightness. I will cast you to the ground; I will put you before kings, that they may behold you."

From the passages of Ezekiel, we see that nothing good comes from self-exaltation and pride. God will surely humble the prideful. They will be brought down to their knees until they repent in humbleness of heart and the Lord restores them. Satan committed the ultimate sin, taking with him multitudes of angels which are now described as demons.

That same spirit is among us today. Many churches have been destroyed because of pride. Many men have decided in their hearts that they were called of God and became "I specialists" instead of waiting on the Lord in humility and patience. Many have launched out in pride and rebellion and have caused much pain for themselves and all that followed them. Paul speaking in 1 Timothy 3:6-7, said the following about a leader who is a novice:

"That a novice, lest being puffed up may fall into the condemnation of the devil." verse 7 says he must also have a good report from those on the outside, lest he fall into reproach and the snare of the devil."

Paul describing the attributes of an overseer or leader stated that one who is a beginner or novice could become puffed up or prideful, and fall into the same state that Satan did. We must understand that God sits high and looks low and sees the humble man as well as the prideful man.

Isaiah 2:11-12 NKJV
(11) The lofty looks of man shall be humbled, The haughtiness of men shall be bowed down, And the LORD alone shall be exalted in that day.
(12) For the day of the LORD of hosts shall come upon everything proud and lofty, upon everything lifted up, and it shall be brought low.

Proverbs 8:13 NKJV
(13) The fear of the LORD is to hate evil, pride and arrogance and the evil way, and the perverse mouth I hate.

From the scriptures above, we see that pride is a hindrance to the blessing of God and it is one of Satan's most popular weapons to use against the people of God, to block your blessing, and to hinder your relationship with Jesus Christ.
Jesus said that no man can snatch you out of my hand, but the enemy is crafty and will use deceptive devices to get God's people out of the perfect will of God. Instead of pride we must follow the example of Christ in which the Apostle Paul said in Phil 2:1-4

Philippians 2:1-4 NKJV

(1) Therefore, if there is any consolation in Christ, if any comfort of love, if any fellowship of the Spirit, if any affection and mercy,
(2) fulfill my joy by being like-minded, having the same love, being of one accord, of one mind.
(3) Let nothing be done through selfish ambition or conceit, but in lowliness of mind let each esteem others better than himself.
(4) Let each of you look out not only for his own interests, but also for the interests of others.

The Lord also taught us that humility is the attitude that we should have.

Matthew 18:1-5 NKJV
(1) At that time the disciples came to Jesus, saying, "Who then is greatest in the kingdom of heaven?"
(2) Then Jesus called a little child to Him, set him in the midst of them,
(3) and said, "Assuredly, I say to you, unless you are converted and become as little children, you will by no means enter the kingdom of heaven.
(4) Therefore, whoever humbles himself as this little child is the greatest in the kingdom of heaven.
(5) Whoever receives one little child like this in My name receives Me.

In this passage of scripture, the LORD shows us that the mindset of humility is that of a child. A child is humble, teachable, correctable, and even must be disciplined sometimes. One characteristic that Jesus continually taught his disciples was humility and how important it was to be a servant. Even as he was in the upper room before he went to the cross, he taught his disciples how to serve one another as he served them communion and even washed the feet of his disciples.

John 13:12-17 NKJV

(12) So, when He had washed their feet, taken His garments, and sat down again, He said to them, "Do you know what I have done to you?
(13) You call Me Teacher and Lord, and you say well, for so I am.
(14) If I then, your Lord and Teacher, have washed your feet, you also ought to wash one another's feet.
(15) For I have given you an example, that you should do as I have done to you.
(16) Most assuredly, I say to you, a servant is not greater than his master; nor is he who is sent greater than he who sent him.
(17) If you know these things, blessed are you if you do them.

Jesus illustrates and demonstrates the attitude of humility and how important it was for the disciples to have a servant's heart. As a matter of fact, today it is equally important that we as the people of God have the same mindset. Even the Lord Jesus Christ set the ultimate example of servitude by humbling himself, and became obedient to the point of death, even the death of the cross according to Phil 2: 8.

"And being found in appearance as a man, He humbled Himself and became obedient to the point of death, even the death of the cross."
Philippians 2:8 NKJV

The Apostle Paul gave Timothy some profound advice concerning the prideful state of man in the last days. I believe that this is exactly the state of the times in which we live today.

2 Timothy 3:1-5 NKJV
(1) But know this, that in the last days perilous times will come:

(2) For men will be lovers of themselves, lovers of money, boasters, proud, blasphemers, disobedient to parents, unthankful, unholy,
(3) unloving, unforgiving, slanderers, without self-control, brutal, despisers of good,
(4) traitors, headstrong, haughty, lovers of pleasure rather than lovers of God,
(5) having a form of godliness but denying its power, and from such people turn away!

   Notice that everything that Paul mentioned has to do with pride, selfishness, and self-righteousness. Aren't these the times in which we live? The selfie generation, the narcissistic generation in which everything we do, it must be showcased.  I mean all you have to do is look around the social media world today and you will find on Facebook, Instagram,  Twitter and other sites that somebody has a quote, somebody has a word, a cliché, a Youtube video, a word of wisdom, a status update, or just anything to say look what I accomplished!

 And the reason is because we want everybody to know what we have done, what we have achieved, how good we look, where we have been, what we are driving, or how smart we are!  Truth be told, I have done it, and you have probably done it as well.
   Deep down inside, we all desire to share what we have achieved, or what we have accomplished, and there is nothing wrong with that,  if you are doing it for the right reason. But we must be careful, because God hates pride according to Prov 6: 17.

Proverbs 6:16-19 NKJV
(16) These six things the LORD hates, yes, seven are an abomination to Him:
(17) **A proud look**, a lying tongue, hands that shed innocent blood,

(18) A heart that devises wicked plans, Feet that are swift in running to evil,
(19) A false witness who speaks lies, And one who sows discord among brethren.

I believe one of the reasons why God hates pride is because Satan uses the prideful nature of man to strengthen his evil kingdom. Pride manifests itself in self-righteousness, positions of power, constant lifting of one's self, self-exaltation, vanity, and a lack of submission to authority.

"A man's pride will bring him low, but the humble in spirit will retain honor."
Proverbs 29:23 NKJV

We find continuously in the scriptures that there is the humble are lifted up and the prideful are brought low. The attitude of humility is a wonderful attitude that each and every person should strive to have, and always maintain. Humility is so important that it can be summed up in the following verse in which the LORD said that he is high and lifted up and inhabits eternity, and dwells in the high and holy place, with those that have a contrite and humble spirit. He also said that he would revive the spirit of the humble, and revive the heart of the contrite ones.

"For thus says the high and lofty One that inhabits eternity, whose name is Holy; I dwell in the high and holy place, with him also that is of a contrite and humble spirit, to revive the spirit of the humble, and to revive the heart of the contrite ones."
Isaiah 57:15 KJV

It is my prayer that we will always have the attitude and mind of Jesus Christ, which is humility. Humility is not weakness, it is meekness. Humility is not about status, what we have achieved, or obtained. Humility is the characteristic that the LORD desires all of his beloved children to have. Pride is a hindrance to the blessing of God, but humility brings honor and the blessing of God!

## SCRIPTURES ON HUMILITY

"The fear of the LORD is the instruction of wisdom, and before honor is humility."
Proverbs 15:33 NKJV

"By humility and the fear of the LORD are riches and honor and life."
Proverbs 22:4 NKJV

"Seek the LORD, all you meek of the earth, who have upheld His justice. Seek righteousness, seek humility. It may be that you will be hidden In the day of the LORD's anger."
Zephaniah 2:3 NKJV

"Therefore, as the elect of God, holy and beloved, put-on tender mercies, kindness, humility, meekness, longsuffering;"
Colossians 3:12 NKJV

"Likewise, ye younger, submit yourselves unto the elder. Yea, all of you be subject one to another, and be clothed with humility: for God resists the proud, and giveth grace to the humble." 1 Peter 5:5 KJV

# CHAPTER 5 - REBELLION

In our previous chapters we have discussed disobedience, idolatry, and pride. We will now discuss the 4th hindrance to the blessing of God, which is rebellion.

"Blessed be the God and Father of our Lord Jesus Christ, who hath blessed us with all spiritual blessings in heavenly places in Christ."
Ephesians 1:3 KJV

How many of us know that according to Ephesians 1: 3 we have been blessed with all spiritual blessings in heavenly places in Christ Jesus! This is one of the reasons why the enemy desires to hinder us in our relationship with the LORD. This is why we should endeavor to abide in that secret place under the shadow of the Almighty. (Psalms 91: 1)

One important thing that we need to understand is that God will not, and cannot go against his Word. The abounding blessings of the Lord belongs to the one who is faithful in obedience, faith, humility, righteousness, holiness, truth, and loves the Lord with all their heart, soul, mind and strength.

"A faithful man will abound with blessings, but he who hastens to be rich will not go unpunished."
Proverbs 28:20 NKJV

One of the things that we must understand is God sends rain on righteous and unrighteous, but his favor and blessing does not rest on anyone who walks in disobedience, idolatry, pride or rebellion. If you study the scriptures you will find that there were many Old and New Testament examples of people that were rebuked, disciplined, and lost their position of leadership, because they walked contrary to the Word of God. The Apostle

Paul goes on to say in 1 Cor 10: 11, "Now all these things happened to them as examples, and they were written for our admonition, upon whom the ends of the ages have come"

Now the scripture states that these things happened as them as examples and they were written for our admonition. The word admonition is defined as; gentle reproof, counseling against a fault, instruction in duties, caution, and direction. It also states that it is used in church discipline as public or private reproof to reclaim an offender.

One thing we must understand is it doesn't matter how long you've been saved, how long you have been in church, who you may be affiliated with, how many degrees you have, or how educated you may be in Bible knowledge, rebellion is a hindrance to the blessing of the Lord, but repentance restores our relationship with the Lord.

I have found while studying the Bible that rebellion is mentioned all throughout the Bible, and is a serious charge to the individuals that choose rebellion, rather than obedience to the Word of God and God's established authority.

What is rebellion? *Webster's online dictionary* defines rebellion as; Opposition to one in authority or dominance, defiance or resistance to established authority, an organized uprising to change, or to overthrow an existing authority.

In our last chapter we read from the books of Isaiah chapter 14 and Ezekiel chapter 28 about the pride of Satan, which caused him to rebel against God and was cast out of heaven. We also looked at King Saul's continued disobedience and the prophetic word that spoken against him by the Prophet Samuel in 1 Samuel 15:23 who said, "For rebellion is as the sin of witchcraft, and stubbornness is as iniquity and idolatry." As a result of Saul's rebellion in rejecting the Word of the LORD, he also was rejected from being king.

But Samuel said to Saul, "I will not return with you, for you have rejected the word of the LORD, and the LORD has rejected you from being king over Israel."
1 Samuel 15:26 NKJV

Isn't it interesting that God compared rebellion to witchcraft? Why did God compare rebellion to witchcraft? Well, the answer is simple. Witchcraft conjures and stirs up evil, and it is an evil spirit of rebellion that stirs the emotions of individuals to rebel against established authority.

The sin that we see today in satanic worship, alternative lifestyles, disobedience, idolatry, and pride is a result of man's rebellion towards God who is the established authority in the universe. Rebellion is a spirit that resists authority and speaks against authority. It is an arrogant spirit, a prideful spirit that says it's my way or the highway.

Rebellion manifests itself in marriages, in children, in the church and anywhere Gods established authority resides. In the Bible the number 13 is associated with rebellion. Maybe this is why 13 is such a superstitious number and is associated with evil.

In Mark 7:21 –23 Jesus mentions 13 things that proceed out of the heart of men which is symbolic of rebellion.
Mark 7:21-23 NKJV
(21) For from within, out of the heart of men, proceed evil thoughts, adulteries, fornications, murders,
(22) thefts, covetousness, wickedness, deceit, lewdness, an evil eye, blasphemy, pride, foolishness.
(23) All these evil things come from within and defile a man."

What is even more interesting is that Paul wrote something very prophetic in Romans 13: 1-5 concerning rebellion and authority.

Romans 13:1-4 NKJV
(1) Let every soul be subject to the governing authorities. For there is no authority except from God, and the authorities that exist are appointed by God.
(2) Therefore, whoever resists the authority resists the ordinance of God, and those who resist will bring judgment on themselves.
(3) For rulers are not a terror to good works, but to evil. Do you want to be unafraid of the authority? Do what is good, and you will have praise from the same.
(4) For he is God's minister to you for good. But if you do evil, be afraid; for he does not bear the sword in vain; for he is God's minister, an avenger to execute wrath on him who practices evil.

The Apostle Paul stated that there is no authority except from God, and the authorities that exist are appointed by God. Authority exists in the earth to maintain order. Sometimes there is authority that produces disorder. This authority has been allowed to rule by God, but it will also be judged by God.

## The Rebellion against Moses

King Solomon wrote in Proverbs 17:11 that an evil man seeks only rebellion; Therefore, a cruel messenger will be sent against him. In the book of Numbers there is a story of Moses and what happens when people rebel against established authority.

Numbers 16:1-4 NKJV

(1) Now Korah the son of Izhar, the son of Kohath, the son of Levi, with Dathan and Abiram the sons of Eliab,

and On the son of Peleth, sons of Reuben, took men;
(2) and they rose up before Moses with some of the
children of Israel, two hundred and fifty leaders of the
congregation, representatives of the congregation, men
of renown.
(3) They gathered together against Moses and Aaron,
and said to them, "You take too much upon yourselves,
for all the congregation is holy, every one of them, and
the LORD is among them. Why then do you exalt
yourselves above the assembly of the LORD?"
(4) So when Moses heard it, he fell on his face.

We find in Numbers chapter 16 that leaders of the
congregation; Korah, Dathan, Abiram and On decided to
rise up against the leadership of Moses. (verse 1 and 2)
The Bible says that they gathered together against Moses
and Aaron with two hundred and fifty leaders of the
congregation saying, "You take too much upon
yourselves, for all the congregation is holy, every one of
them, and the LORD is among them. Why then do you
exalt yourselves above the assembly of the LORD?"
For some reason or another they did not respect the
leadership of Moses. Notice the language that they use in
verse 3. This is where rebellion begins. The individuals
most of the time are leaders, or those that believe that
the current leadership is not worthy to respect or to
follow.

They then begin to make statements about the
leadership to other leaders through gossip, accusations,
slander and condemnation. Instead of voicing their
opinions in a respectful way through a meeting or
dialogue if they have a valid complaint or concern, the
Bible says they rose up before Moses! In other words,
they were saying, "Moses who do you think you are?"
We are all holy! We are all anointed and the LORD is
among us all in the congregation. They were in essence
saying, "Moses, you are not the only person that hears

from the LORD!" The Bible then says that Moses fell on his face in Numbers 16:4.

Can you imagine how Moses felt? He is the leader of the children of Israel. The people are murmuring and complaining against him. He is doing his best to lead them, and in the midst of it all, they begin to dishonor and disrespect him. Moses then responds in verses 8-15:

Numbers 16:8-15 NKJV
(8) Then Moses said to Korah, "Hear now, you sons of Levi:
(9) Is it a small thing to you that the God of Israel has separated you from the congregation of Israel, to bring you near to Himself, to do the work of the tabernacle of the LORD, and to stand before the congregation to serve them,
(10) and that He has brought you near to Himself, you and all your brethren, the sons of Levi, with you? And are you seeking the priesthood also?
(11) Therefore, you and all your company are gathered together against the LORD. And what is Aaron that you complain against him?"
(12) And Moses sent to call Dathan and Abiram the sons of Eliab, but they said, "We will not come up!
(13) Is it a small thing that you have brought us up out of a land flowing with milk and honey, to kill us in the wilderness, that you should keep acting like a prince over us?
(14) Moreover, you have not brought us into a land flowing with milk and honey, nor given us inheritance of fields and vineyards. Will you put out the eyes of these men? We will not come up!"
(15) Then Moses was very angry, and said to the LORD, "Do not respect their offering. I have not taken one donkey from them, nor have I hurt one of them."

In the midst of the rebellion, Moses defends himself

and Aaron. He even tries to reconcile by calling the leaders of the rebellion to discuss the situation.
The Bible says that they responded by saying in verse 12, "We will not come up!" Then they proceed to say additional negative things about Moses leadership since they left Egypt.

Isn't this amazing? Here we have men who are of the tribe of Levi. They are leaders among the congregation and they have decided that Moses is not hearing from God. He is not a good leader, and he brought them into the wilderness to die.
They then reiterate in verse 15, "We will not come up!" Wow, can you see the disobedience, pride, rebellion, anger and resentment against God's established leadership?

Brothers and Sisters who may be reading this chapter, one of the worse mistakes you can ever make is to rebel against the legitimate established authority of God. Moses was God's man. He selected Moses and Aaron to lead the children of Israel out of Egypt into the Promised Land, and to rebel against Moses was to rebel against God's established authority! Moses defended himself by saying in verse 15, "I have not taken one donkey from them, nor have I hurt one of them."

When you read the rest of the chapter in Numbers 16: 16-35, we find that Moses charges each man that rebelled to come with him to the door of the Tabernacle of Meeting to appear before the LORD.

The LORD passes judgment on their rebellion and all of them are consumed by the glory of the LORD. Korah, Dathan, Abiram, their families and all their belongings were swallowed up into the earth, and the LORD sent a fire and consumed the two hundred fifty leaders of the congregation who rebelled against Moses.

Numbers 16:31-35 NKJV

(31) Now it came to pass, as he finished speaking all these words, that the ground split apart under them, (32) and the earth opened its mouth and swallowed them up, with their households and all the men with Korah, with all their goods.

(33) So, they and all those with them went down alive into the pit; the earth closed over them, and they perished from among the assembly.

(34) Then all Israel who were around them fled at their cry, for they said, "Lest the earth swallow us up also!"

(35) And a fire came out from the LORD and consumed the two hundred and fifty men who were offering incense.

One thing that we should never do is resist the authority of God. We live in a time where people have taken on the spirit of the world, in which they think they can say or do anything they want to God's established leadership. People in church today have taken on the spirit of democracy which is the rule of the people, when we live in a theocracy which is the rule of God in the Kingdom of God.

We must never allow the things of the world to dictate how we do things in the house of God and in our homes. Everything that we do in the house of God should be according to the Word of God. In our homes, in our personal lives, how we raise our children, and everything that pertains to life and Godliness.

When we do things according to the Word of God and the established order of God, the blessing of the Lord is released upon our lives. When we do things according to the world, or of our own volition we set ourselves up for failure.

"And do not be conformed to this world, but be

transformed by the renewing of your mind, that you may prove what is that good and acceptable and perfect will of God."
Romans 12:2 NKJV

There is no way that we can live rebellious lives and expect God to bless the work and fruit of our hands. As Kingdom citizens in Christ, we must be transformed by the renewing of our minds, which means that we have the mind of Christ and not the mind of the world.

Ephesians 4:21-24 NKJV
(21) if indeed you have heard Him and have been taught by Him, as the truth is in Jesus:
(22) that you put off, concerning your former conduct, the old man which grows corrupt according to the deceitful lusts,
(23) and be renewed in the spirit of your mind,
(24) and that you put on the new man which was created according to God, in true righteousness and holiness.

If we are going to make a difference in the world for the Kingdom of God, we need to walk according to the Word of God. Instead of a rebellious spirit, we should always have the spirit of humility and submission which is a great attribute in the Kingdom of God.

King David was a man of great humility and his life and attitude is a pattern for us to follow. When he was anointed King of Israel to take King Saul's place, King Saul was furious and attempted to kill him. He chased David all over Israel trying to kill him but David just kept on running and would never speak against King Saul. Finally, when David had the opportunity to kill King Saul look what he said in 1 Samuel 24: 10-12:

(10) Look, this day your eyes have seen that the LORD delivered you today into my hand in the cave, and someone urged me to kill you. But my eye spared you,

and I said, 'I will not stretch out my hand against my lord, for he is the LORD's anointed.'

(11) Moreover, my father, see! Yes, see the corner of your robe in my hand! For in that I cut off the corner of your robe, and did not kill you, know and see that there is neither evil nor rebellion in my hand, and I have not sinned against you. Yet you hunt my life to take it.

(12) Let the LORD judge between you and me, and let the LORD avenge me on you. But my hand shall not be against you.

The difference between Korah and Moses and David and King Saul is this:
Korah rebelled against Moses and spoke against him. He took 250 men with him and they all rose up against Moses and Aaron. As a result, 14,700 people lost their lives!

David would not touch or speak a word against King Saul even when Gods' anointing was lifted off of him. David had the opportunity to kill King Saul and would have been justified in doing so, but he knew that the battle was not his, but the Lords.'

I want to share something with you. If you have ever been hurt by someone in authority, leave it with God, turn it over to God. For God is the judge and will judge righteously.

Maybe this is why David is a type of Christ, or his life is symbolic of Jesus Christ. He showed great restraint and humility even when he could have defended himself.

## Jesus in the Garden of Gethsemane

When Judas and the soldiers came to arrest Jesus in the Garden of Gethsemane they came with swords and clubs and Jesus said something profound to Peter in Matthew 26:52-53:

(52) But Jesus said to him, "Put your sword in its place, for all who take the sword will perish by the sword. (53) Or do you think that I cannot now pray to My Father, and He will provide Me with more than twelve legions of angels?

Jesus understood that this was the will of God as he as preparing to go to the cross. Peter wanted to fight and defend Jesus, but Jesus knew that this was part of the journey. Jesus also made the statement that if he wanted to fight, he could call a legion of angels to defend him!

A legion consisted of 3, 000 – 6,000 Roman troops. So, Jesus was saying that he could pray to his father, and his father could send up to 72,000 warring angels. Wow! Am I saying let people walk over you, or take advantage of you? By no means, because we should never ever let people take advantage of us because we are meek.  As believers in Christ, we are called to be meek but definitely not weak!

Sometimes we do things in the flesh that only escalates a situation. We need more patience and longsuffering which is the fruit of the spirit. Jesus said that if your neighbor compels you to go one mile, go two miles. (Matt 5: 41)  We need more two-mile believers in the Body of Christ who can go the distance in patience with others. We are so quick to brush people aside nowadays, but that's not what Christ taught us. One of the fruit of the spirit is long suffering which means patience or able to bear long.   Listen to the testimony of Jesus Christ:

Isaiah 53:5-7 NKJV
(5) But He was wounded for our transgressions, He was

bruised for our iniquities; The chastisement for our peace was upon Him, And by His stripes we are healed. (6) All we like sheep have gone astray; We have turned, every one, to his own way; And the LORD has laid on Him the iniquity of us all.

**(7) He was oppressed and He was afflicted, Yet He opened not His mouth; He was led as a lamb to the slaughter, and as a sheep before its shearers is silent, So He opened not His mouth.**

When we humble ourselves and submit to established authority, we are submitting to Gods authority whether it is in the home, church, work, school or wherever there is leadership. We should never ever submit to anything that is wrong or immoral, or does not line up with the Word of God. But when we submit to righteous authority, we submit to the authority of God. When we do that, I believe that God's grace, mercy and blessing will shield us, cover us and protect us from all hurt, harm and danger.

God in his sovereignty has given us the freedom to choose. We must remember that God knows the choices we will make but still gives us the ability to make a choice. If we are willing and obedient, we shall eat the good of the land. In other words, you will reap the abundant blessings of God.  If we refuse and rebel, we will be devoured by the sword. In other words, we will not reap the good, but rather divine discipline or destruction.

It is much more to our advantage to walk hand in hand with God, to submit to authority, parents and leaders that God places in our midst. Continued disobedience ultimately leads to a state of rebellion. Continued rebellion ultimately leads to spiritual death unless one repents and submits to the Lord.

## Attitude is the Key

We obtain the blessing through submission to Gods established authority and those that God has appointed over us. God's established authority is anyone that God has placed over us in the home, the church, the workplace and in government. We cannot carelessly rebel against authority. God takes notice of our attitudes, words and actions.

I am not saying that we should submit to all authority, because there is evil authority in the world that goes against the Word of God. When authority violates scripture, we must follow scripture. We can never go wrong went we follow the Word of God.

We must be careful not to participate in anything that is ungodly, unholy, unrighteous or untrue. A spirit of submission is the proper attitude to maintain at all times. When we submit to authority, we submit to God. For the Bible states in Romans 13: 1-5:

Romans 13:1-5 NKJV
(1) Let every soul be subject to the governing authorities. For there is no authority except from God, and the authorities that exist are appointed by God.
(2) Therefore, whoever resists the authority resists the ordinance of God, and those who resist will bring judgment on themselves.
(3) For rulers are not a terror to good works, but to evil. Do you want to be unafraid of the authority? Do what is good, and you will have praise from the same.
(4) For he is God's minister to you for good. But if you do evil, be afraid; for he does not bear the sword in vain; for he is God's minister, an avenger to execute wrath on him who practices evil.
(5) Therefore, you must be subject, not only because of wrath but also for conscience' sake.

Verse 3 states that rulers are not a terror to good works, but to evil. Do what is good, and you shall have praise from the same. In other words, do what good in the sight of the Lord, submit to God's legitimate established authority, and watch God bless your life abundantly.

Out of all the hindrances that we have discussed, the one that sticks out most in my mind is unbelief. Unbelief can be defined as doubt or the absence of faith. Unbelief also comes from fear. I believe that every sin ultimately starts with the sin of unbelief.
All of the hindrances are equally unacceptable to the Lord, but throughout scripture I find that one of the greatest hindrances to the blessings of God is unbelief.

Unbelief is a lack of faith in what God has promised and spoken in his Word. Numbers 23: 19 says it this way, "God is not a man that He should lie, neither the son of man that He should repent. Has He said, and shall He not do it? Or has He spoken, and shall He not make it good?" God's word is true and his promises are yes and amen. What God has said in his word will surely come to pass. Not in our time or when we think that it will come to pass, but in God's sovereign timing, because God's word will never fall to the ground. It may be delayed until the appropriate time and season, but it shall come to pass at the appointed time.

## The Writer of Hebrews Speaks about Unbelief

Hebrews 3:7-19 KJV
(7)  Wherefore (as the Holy Ghost says, today if ye will hear his voice,
(8)  Harden not your hearts, as in the provocation, in the day of temptation in the wilderness:
(9)  When your fathers tempted me, proved me, and saw my works forty years.
(10)  Wherefore I was grieved with that generation, and said, they do always err in their heart; and they have not known my ways.
(11)  So, I swore in my wrath, they shall not enter into my rest.

**(12) Take heed, brethren, lest there be in any of you an evil heart of unbelief, in departing from the living God.**

(13) But exhort one another daily, while it is called today; lest any of you be hardened through the deceitfulness of sin.

(14) For we are made partakers of Christ, if we hold the beginning of our confidence steadfast unto the end;

(15) While it is said, today if ye will hear his voice, harden not your hearts, as in the provocation.

(16) For some, when they had heard, did provoke: howbeit not all that came out of Egypt by Moses.

(17) But with whom was he grieved forty years? Was it not with them that had sinned, whose carcasses fell in the wilderness?

(18) And to whom sware he that they should not enter into his rest, but to them that believed not?

(19) So, we see that they could not enter in because of unbelief.

We know that the writer of Hebrews was referring to the Israelites in the Old Testament who journeyed through the desert, murmuring, complaining, and griping against the leadership of Moses and Aaron, and God was not pleased with them.

Hebrews 3: 8-11 gives us some insight as to why God was angry with that generation of people, and said they will never enter his rest. He also exhorts us as New Testament believers to learn from their example, by saying in verse 12, take heed  brethren, lest there be in any of you an evil heart of unbelief  in departing from the living God. The writer is clearly giving us a warning not to have a spirit of unbelief,  because without faith it is impossible to please God according to Hebrew 11: 6.

# A Profound Old Testament Example of Unbelief

In Numbers chapter 13 you can read about why God was angry with the children of Israel. In Numbers 13, The LORD told Moses to send 12 spies into the land that he was giving them. Two out of twelve people believed God. Ten men didn't believe God, because of the giants they saw in the land. When they saw these giants they feared, and began to doubt that they could overcome them. They even saw themselves as grasshoppers compared to the giants. Now we must understand that it was the LORD in Numbers 13 that gave Moses the command to spy out the land he was giving to them.

"And the LORD spoke to Moses, saying, "Send men to spy out the land of Canaan, which I am giving to the children of Israel; from each tribe of their fathers, you shall send a man, everyone a leader among them." Numbers 13:1-2 NKJV

Did you read what God said? Send men to spy out the land of Canaan, which I am giving to the children of Israel. In other words, it was already done. They just had to be obedient! The Bible says, "God calls those things that be not as though they are" (Rom 4: 17). In other words, God had already purposed they would take possession of the land, if they had faith in his word to spy it out, and take possession of it, they would enter in. The Bible says that after forty days of spying out the land, they came back with a negative report. Listen to what their report was:

Numbers 13:25-29 NKJV
25 And they returned from spying out the land after forty days.
26 Now they departed and came back to Moses and Aaron and all the congregation of the children of Israel in the Wilderness of Paran, at Kadesh; they brought back

word to them and to all the congregation, and showed them the fruit of the land.

27 Then they told him, and said: "We went to the land where you sent us. It truly flows with milk and honey, and this is its fruit.

28 Nevertheless the people who dwell in the land are strong; the cities are fortified and very large; moreover we saw the descendants of Anak there.

29 The Amalekites dwell in the land of the South; the Hittites, the Jebusites, and the Amorites dwell in the mountains; and the Canaanites dwell by the sea and along the banks of the Jordan."

Now what is interesting is that God had already said that he is giving them the land, yet ten men did not believe the report of the LORD. Only two people believed the Word of the LORD; Joshua and Caleb. Let's read what they said after spying out the land for forty days. Numbers 13:30-33 NKJV

(30) Then Caleb quieted the people before Moses, and said, "Let us go up at once and take possession, for we are well able to overcome it."

(31) But the men who had gone up with him said, "We are not able to go up against the people, for they are stronger than we."

(32) And they gave the children of Israel a bad report of the land which they had spied out, saying, "The land through which we have gone as spies is a land that devours its inhabitants, and all the people whom we saw in it are men of great stature.

(33) There we saw the giants (the descendants of Anak came from the giants); and we were like grasshoppers in our own sight, and so we were in their sight."

Because of fear, doubt and unbelief, an evil report was stirred up amongst the people by the ten men. (Numbers 13: 32) Their disobedience and unwillingness to take possession of the land caused many of them to not enter into the Promised Land.

Numbers 14:22-23 NKJV
(22) because all these men who have seen My glory and the signs which I did in Egypt and in the wilderness, and have put Me to the test now these ten times, and have not heeded My voice,
(23) they certainly shall not see the land of which I swore to their fathers, nor shall any of those who rejected Me see it.

Listen to what the Bible says about Caleb's obedience. "But my servant Caleb, because he had another spirit in him, and has followed me fully, him will I bring into the land where into he went, and his seed shall possess it." (Numbers 14: 24)

One of the greatest hindrances to the blessings of God is unbelief.  Lack of faith in what God has promised and spoken.   God's word is true and his promises are yes and amen. When God speaks a word you can believe that it shall come to pass. Not in our time or when we think that it will come to pass, but in the appropriate season and appointed time.

We must trust God's Word entirely and not waiver on the promises of God. Walking in unbelief could be detrimental to our spiritual growth, so the writer of Hebrews exhorts us to learn from the mistakes of those that came before us.
Although the LORD had given them the land they did not enter in because of unbelief.  Listen to the admonishment of the Hebrews writer.

Hebrews 4:1-3 KJV
(1) Let us therefore fear, lest, a promise being left us of entering into his rest, any of you should seem to come

short of it.

(2) For unto us was the gospel preached, as well as unto them, but the word preached did not profit them, not being mixed with faith in them that heard it.

(3) For we which have believed do enter into rest, as he said, as I have sworn in my wrath, if they shall enter into my rest: although the works were finished from the foundation of the world.

The writer says that the gospel (good news) was preached unto them as well, but it did not profit them. Because they did not mix the hearing of God's Word with faith! Therefore, God said, "You will not enter into my rest." He then ends with the admonishment; "Let us labor therefore to enter into that rest, lest any man fall after the same example of unbelief." (Hebrews 4: 11) This New Testament warning is profound because we should endeavor to enter into God's rest through faith and trusting God's Word.

So, we see that hearing the Word needs to be mixed with faith. Maybe that's why Paul said in Rom 10:17, "So then faith comes by hearing, and hearing by the word of God."

Question? What is your response when you hear the Word of God from God's servants? Do you receive it with joy or do you challenge it?

God uses human vessels to teach and preach his Word in the earth! When we receive a man or woman of God in Jesus Name, we receive a just reward because of our belief in that office or ministry in Jesus Christ.

"He who receives you receives Me, and he who receives Me receives Him who sent Me. He who receives a prophet in the name of a prophet shall receive a prophet's reward. And he who receives a righteous man in the name of a righteous man shall receive a righteous man's reward." Matthew 10:40-41 NKJV

"How then shall they call on him in whom they have not believed? And how shall they believe in him of whom they have not heard? And how shall they hear without a preacher? And how shall they preach, except they be sent? As it is written, how beautiful are the feet of them that preach the gospel of peace, and bring glad tidings of good things!"
Romans 10:14-15 KJV

When we receive a true man or woman of God in Jesus Name, we receive a just reward because of our belief in that man or woman's ministry in Jesus Christ. Only those with teachable and humble hearts can discern the hand of the Lord upon his servants and receive from them. Even today, many people don't believe the Word that is spoken from the pulpit, and the gift that is bestowed upon Gods servants. Only through faith can we trust God's word entirely and completely.

Many people miss God because of the package that proclaims God's word. It may be a denominational hindrance, traditional hindrance, or a gender hindrance such as a woman preacher, but regardless of the hindrance, walking in unbelief can be a hindrance to our spiritual growth in the Lord.

### The Unbelief in Jesus Hometown

Mark 6:1-6 NKJV
(1) Then He went out from there and came to His own country, and His disciples followed Him.
(2) And when the Sabbath had come, He began to teach in the synagogue. And many hearing Him were astonished, saying, "Where did this Man get these things? And what wisdom is this which is given to Him, that such mighty works are performed by His hands!"

(3) Is this not the carpenter, the Son of Mary, and brother of James, Joses, Judas, and Simon? And are not His sisters here with us?" So they were offended at Him. (4) But Jesus said to them, "A prophet is not without honor except in his own country, among his own relatives, and in his own house."

**(5) Now He could do no mighty work there, except that He laid His hands on a few sick people and healed them.**

**(6) And He marveled because of their unbelief. Then He went about the villages in a circuit, teaching.**

Isn't this amazing? Jesus came to his own country among the people he knew, and they were astonished at his teaching and wisdom. Jesus must have been doing some profound revelational teaching because they asked the question, "Where did this Man get these things? And what wisdom is this which is given to Him, that such mighty works are performed by His hands!" (Verse 2)

What is even more amazing is that they said, "Is this not the carpenter, the Son of Mary, and brother of James, Joses, Judas, and Simon? And are not His sisters here with us?" So, they were offended at Him! This is the most interesting thing that I have ever read in the Gospels because the Bible says that, "Jesus could do no mighty works there, and he was only able to lay hands on a few sick people and healed them." The scripture also says that he marveled because of their unbelief! (Verse 5-6)

I can relate to what the scripture says because as a Pastor, many times there are friends and family members who can't believe that my wife and I have been called to Pastor and lead a church!

The Bible says that Jesus marveled at the unbelief of those that knew him, and he could do no mighty work there!

Mark 6: 1-6 tells me one thing, that the power of God is activated by faith in God!  The people had no faith, and could not believe that Jesus was doing all those mighty works.

As a matter of fact, they were offended! Isn't it amazing that some people who you grew up with, or knew you back then, cannot accept the fact that God is doing a mighty work in you, which in fact has little to do with you!  Brothers and Sisters, we should always remember that it is not the individual that is doing the work of God, but it is the Holy Spirit who does the work. We are only vessels to be used for the glory of God.

 In the New Testament book of Luke 1 there are examples that have been set before us as well. Many of us know the story of Mary and Elizabeth. Mary was the mother of Jesus, Elizabeth was the mother of John the Baptist, the forerunner of Jesus!  But what is interesting is that they both were experiencing something supernatural that could not be explained in the natural.
    Elizabeth was barren, and Mary had never been with a man, but they were both impregnated with a seed of promise of child through a prophetic word from the LORD. When Elizabeth's husband, Zechariah received a prophetic word from the angel of the LORD that his wife would have a male child, he couldn't believe it!  As a result, his mouth was shut for a season, because he did not believe the report of the Lord that Elizabeth would bear him a son although she was barren.

Luke 1:11-20 NKJV
(11) Then an angel of the Lord appeared to him, standing on the right side of the altar of incense.
(12) And when Zacharias saw him, he was troubled, and fear fell upon him.
(13) But the angel said to him, "Do not be afraid, Zacharias, for your prayer is heard; and your wife

Elizabeth will bear you a son, and you shall call his name John.

(14) And you will have joy and gladness, and many will rejoice at his birth.

(15) For he will be great in the sight of the Lord, and shall drink neither wine nor strong drink. He will also be filled with the Holy Spirit, even from his mother's womb.

(16) And he will turn many of the children of Israel to the Lord their God.

(17) He will also go before Him in the spirit and power of Elijah, 'to turn the hearts of the Fathers to the children,' and the disobedient to the wisdom of the just, to make ready a people prepared for the Lord."

(18) And Zacharias said to the angel, "How shall I know this? For I am an old man, and my wife is well advanced in years."

(19) And the angel answered and said to him, "I am Gabriel, who stands in the presence of God, and was sent to speak to you and bring you these glad tidings.

(20) But behold, you will be mute and not able to speak until the day these things take place, because you did not believe my words which will be fulfilled in their own time."

It is interesting to note that because Zacharias that did not receive the prophetic word from the Lord, he entered into a season of delay. His mouth was shut until the set time of John's birth prophesied by the Angel of the Lord. It is the same with us. When we receive a prophetic utterance from God, we must trust God that his Word is true.

We must then believe it, receive it, and walk in it. When we don't believe and walk in unbelief, we question Gods omnipotence and ability to perform what he said he would do. In that same chapter of Luke chapter 1, Mary the Mother of Jesus received a visitation from the Angel of the Lord (Gabriel) as well in Luke 1: 26-38.

Luke 1:26-38 NKJV

(26) Now in the sixth month the angel Gabriel was sent by God to a city of Galilee named Nazareth,
(27) to a virgin betrothed to a man whose name was Joseph, of the house of David. The virgin's name was Mary.
(28) And having come in, the angel said to her, "Rejoice, highly favored one, the Lord is with you; blessed are you among women!"
(29) But when she saw him, she was troubled at his saying, and considered what manner of greeting this was.
(30) Then the angel said to her, "Do not be afraid, Mary, for you have found favor with God.
(31) And behold, you will conceive in your womb and bring forth a Son, and shall call His name JESUS.
(32) He will be great, and will be called the Son of the Highest; and the Lord God will give Him the throne of His father David.
(33) And He will reign over the house of Jacob forever, and of His kingdom there will be no end."
(34) Then Mary said to the angel, "How can this be, since I do not know a man?"
(35) And the angel answered and said to her, "The Holy Spirit will come upon you, and the power of the Highest will overshadow you; therefore, also, that Holy One who is to be born will be called the Son of God.
(36) Now indeed, Elizabeth your relative has also conceived a son in her old age; and this is now the sixth month for her who was called barren.
(37) For with God nothing will be impossible."
(38) Then Mary said, "Behold the maidservant of the Lord! Let it be to me according to your word." And the angel departed from her.

As we contrast these two prophetic visitations from the angel Gabriel, we find two different responses. Zacharias' mouth was shut up for a season because of his unbelief. His response was, "How shall I know this? For I am an old man, and my wife is well advanced in years." (Verse 18) Mary was troubled at first, but she received the word with gladness and told Gabriel in verse 38, "Behold the maidservant of the Lord! Let it be to me according to your word." And the angel departed from her.

The difference between a delayed blessing and a "now" blessing is walking in faith or unbelief. When we stand on God's spoken and written word we can be sure that God's promises will come to past. The delayed blessing will also come to pass after a time and season, and for some it may also mean a trip to the wilderness to get you back on track.

Child of God you will never receive the promises of God and fulfill the divine purpose in your life until you acknowledge by faith what God has spoken in his Word is true!  When Zacharias acknowledged by faith the word spoken to him by the Angel Gabriel concerning Elizabeth, his tongue was immediately loosed.

Luke 1:59-64 NKJV
(59) So it was, on the eighth day, that they came to circumcise the child; and they would have called him by the name of his father, Zacharias.
(60) His mother answered and said, "No; he shall be called John."
(61) But they said to her, "There is no one among your relatives who is called by this name."
(62) So, they made signs to his father--what he would have him called.
(63) And he asked for a writing tablet, and wrote, saying, "His name is John." So, they all marveled.
(64) Immediately his mouth was opened and his tongue loosed, and he spoke, praising God.

Gabriel told Mary in Luke 1:37, "For with God, nothing will be impossible." Notice that Gabriel said that nothing will be impossible. I want you to know that he was not only speaking to Mary, but to each and every one of us down through the ages that God's omnipotent Word will never fall to the ground.

In the world today, the Word of God is being preached in so many ways. Never in the history of man has there been such a boom in telecommunications and multi-media, with such a vast explosion of knowledge. We have multiple Christian television stations broadcasting the Gospel all over the United States. There are churches on just about every street or corner in our cities, and the Gospel is being preached all over the world. It is evident that the LORD desires that none would perish.

Everyone in the entire world will be able to hear the Gospel of the Lord Jesus Christ in one way or another, so when God judges no one will be without excuse. No one will be able to say, I didn't know, or I didn't have the chance to believe or repent.

"And this gospel of the kingdom will be preached in all the world as a witness to all the nations, and then the end will come."
Matthew 24:14 NKJV

Jesus even saved a man on the cross while he was dying. In his own hour of death, the man said to Jesus, "Lord, remember me when You come into Your kingdom. And Jesus said to him, truly I say to you, today you shall be with me in Paradise."
Luke 23: 42-43 NKJV

Jesus told that man "today" you shall be with me in paradise. He didn't say tomorrow, he didn't say when I come back again. He said TODAY you shall be with me in paradise. One man cursed him; the other man humbled himself, believed God and asked Jesus to remember him.

The Bible says: "For God resists proud ones, but gives grace to the humble." (1 Peter 5:5)

People of God, remember God knows what you need just when you need it. Unbelief in a spiritual sense ultimately comes from not receiving the Word that comes from God. Unbelief can ultimately lead us to miss God and his blessings that he so graciously desires to give. It can also lead to disobedience and rebellion enabling us to fall out of fellowship with God.

Many believers' miscarriage their destiny because of unbelief, God will surely bring to pass that which he has spoken. Although we don't see it, we should trust and believe what the Lord has promised in his word.

2 Cor 5:7 says, "For we walk by faith, not by sight." We must trust God in every area of our life, even when it doesn't look good, feel good, or sound good. We cannot give up, or throw in the towel! Keep trusting God, keep believing God, keep praying, and above all keep praising. Even in Churches today, we must believe what God said that he is going to do. Sometimes we get stuck in observation mode, when God wants us to operate in faith mode. If we really believe that God called us, we must walk by faith, and not by sight, doubt, fear or unbelief.

Hebrews 11:1-2 KJV
(1) Now faith is the substance of things hoped for, the evidence of things not seen.
(2) For by it the elders obtained a good report.
What we need in this time and season is some now faith! We need the faith of God to raise our children, we need the faith of God to advance the Kingdom, we need the faith of God to evangelize, and we need the faith of God to launch out into the deep. Someone once said if you want to walk on water, you have got to get out of the boat.

Some of us are in the boat of comfortability in our lives! The boat is our comfort zone. But God said it's time to get out of the boat and out of your comfort zone. If you want to please God you've got to walk by faith and not by sight. It's time to go from strength to strength and from glory to glory!

It's time to believe God for something new, something fresh, something great, something big, something out of the ordinary, something out of the box, something off the shelf, and something out of sight! One of the most profound scriptures on faith can be found in Mar 11: 24; "Therefore I say to you, whatever things you ask when you pray, believe that you receive them, and you will have them."

## The Ultimate Example of Unbelief

## John 6:47-66

In the book of John 6: 47-66, the ultimate example of unbelief occurred shortly after Jesus proclaimed in verse 48 that he was the Bread of Life. As Jesus was teaching the people, he said something that sparked a controversy amongst those that followed him.
In John 6: 53, the Bible says, "Then Jesus says to them, Truly, truly, I say to you, Unless you eat the flesh of the Son of Man, and drink His blood, you do not have life in yourselves."

When they had heard this they said in John 6:60, "Then when they had heard, many of His disciples said, This is a hard saying, who can hear it?" Jesus then stated in John 6:63; It is the Spirit that makes alive, the flesh profits nothing. The words that I speak to you are spirit and are life. (John 6:64) But there are some of you who do not believe. For Jesus knew from the beginning who they were who did not believe, and who is the one betraying Him.

Right after this, one of the most disappointing verses of scripture ever written  in scripture is recorded in John 6: 66, "From that time many of his disciples went back, and walked no more with him."  I call John 6:66 the man verse! We all know what 666 represents, but look what it says, "Many of his disciples went back and walked no more with him." In other words, they left Jesus Christ and followed him no more. Is this not the ultimate example of unbelief? To hear the word of God, to walk with God and to turn back, and follow him no more! Those that chose to walk with him no more were unbelieving and unconvinced, not understanding what Jesus Christ had just proclaimed in his word.

Sometimes a hard word spoken to those who claim to love us and follow us can expose the real motives behind what they do. Just say something that seems as though it came from outer space, and people who really do not have your heart will take a step in a different direction!

When we say something that people don't agree with or like, they will look at us like Zechariah looked at the Angel Gabriel when he foretold of his wife's impending pregnancy in old age!  Simon Peter's response to the Lord Jesus Christ was monumental when the Lord said to the twelve who remained.  "Then Jesus said to the twelve, "Do you also want to go away?" (John 6:67 NKJV)

Peter replied in John 6:68,  "Lord, to whom shall we go?" You have the Words of eternal life." Isn't this the most profound statement that has ever been uttered by a human being?  When all others forsake you, there are always a few individuals who will trust, believe, and walk with you to the very end. Peter then said, "Also we have come to believe and know that you are the Christ, the Son of the living God." (John 6:69 NKJV)

## Faith is the Key to Receiving God's Blessings and Promises

The pinnacle scripture that turned Catholicism upside down and sparked a reformation and revival that led to Protestantism, was Martin Luther's inspiration from the scriptures, that the just shall live by faith!

Behold, his soul which is lifted up is not upright in him: but the just shall live by his faith.
Habakkuk 2:4 KJV

For unto us was the gospel preached, as well as unto them: but the word preached did not profit them, not being mixed with faith in them that heard it.
Hebrews 4:2 KJV

But without faith it is impossible to please him: for he that cometh to God must believe that he is, and that he is a rewarder of them that diligently seek him.
Hebrews 11:6 KJV

It is truly impossible to please God with anything other than a faith filled believing heart. When we trust God and believe, we can be rest assured that God will reward those who diligently seek him.  Although we don't see it, we trust and believe what the Lord has promised in his word, because Jesus Christ is the same yesterday, today and forevermore.

# CHAPTER 7- UNFORGIVENESS

 Another hindrance to the blessing of God is unforgiveness toward one another.  If there is clearly any one thing in the Bible that will hinder our walk and relationship with the Lord, it is to walk in unforgiveness. To walk in unforgiveness is to clearly walk in contradiction to the teachings of our Lord Jesus Christ. One thing we find in the Scriptures is that whenever Jesus talked about prayer, he associated forgiveness with it. Let's look at the LORD's prayer.

Matthew 6:9-15 NKJV
(9) In this manner, therefore, pray: Our Father in heaven, Hallowed be Your name.
(10) Your kingdom come. Your will be done on earth as it is in heaven.
(11) Give us this day our daily bread.
(12) And forgive us our debts, As we forgive our debtors.
(13) And do not lead us into temptation, But deliver us from the evil one. For yours is the kingdom and the power and the glory forever. Amen.
(14) "For if you forgive men their trespasses, your heavenly Father will also forgive you.
**(15) But if you do not forgive men their trespasses, neither will your Father forgive your trespasses.**
     Peter once asked the Lord, "How many times should I forgive my neighbor who sins against me, seven times? Peter must have known that seven is a perfect and complete number, so he figured that if he forgave seven times it was enough!  It was an interesting question which gave Jesus Christ the opportunity to expound upon the importance of forgiveness.

"Then came Peter to him, and said, Lord, how oft shall my brother sin against me, and I forgive him? Till seven times? Jesus saith unto him, I say not unto thee, until

seven times: but, until seventy times seven."
Matthew 18:21-22 KJV

Jesus answered that seven times would not be enough to forgive your brother or sister, but seventy times seven. This does not mean 490 times is enough, although it quite a lot of forgiveness. It literally means that there can be no number sufficient enough to forgive and release another person from his debt or offense toward you.

## The Parable of the Unforgiving Servant

The parable of the unforgiving servant is a great story of the mercy and forgiveness of our Lord, and how we should follow his example as it relates to forgiveness. Let's take a look:

Matthew 18:23-35 NKJV
(23) Therefore, the kingdom of heaven is like a certain king who wanted to settle accounts with his servants.
(24) And when he had begun to settle accounts, one was brought to him who owed him ten thousand talents.
(25) But as he was not able to pay, his master commanded that he be sold, with his wife and children and all that he had, and that payment be made.
(26) The servant therefore fell down before him, saying, 'Master, have patience with me, and I will pay you all.'
(27) Then the master of that servant was moved with compassion, released him, and forgave him the debt.
(28) "But that servant went out and found one of his fellow servants who owed him a hundred denarii; and he laid hands on him and took him by the throat, saying, 'Pay me what you owe!'
(29) So, his fellow servant fell down at his feet and begged him, saying, 'Have patience with me, and I will pay you all.'
(30) And he would not, but went and threw him into prison till he should pay the debt.

(31)So when his fellow servants saw what had been done, they were very grieved, and came and told their master all that had been done.

(32) Then his master, after he had called him, said to him, 'You wicked servant! I forgave you all that debt because you begged me.

(33) Should you not also have had compassion on your fellow servant, just as I had pity on you?'

(34) And his master was angry, and delivered him to the torturers until he should pay all that was due to him.

(35) "So, My heavenly Father also will do to you if each of you, from his heart, does not forgive his brother his trespasses."

This is a profound story that shows us that we are like that servant at times. God has forgiven us of our sins, but we find it hard to forgive others. The LORD has paid a heavy sin debt on our behalf at the cross and it was a heavy debt indeed.

Yet, many people find it hard to forgive and release others for a small debt or trespass against them! Let's be real! Sometimes it is very hard to forgive and release those that have wounded us with words, lied on us, mistreated us and taken our friendship for granted. Yet, the LORD said to forgive them even as I have forgiven you!

In the parable of the unforgiving servant, his master took him to task and asked in verse 33, "Should you not also have had compassion on your fellow servant, just as I had pity on you?" Isn't this a profound question? If God has shown us mercy, we should show mercy! If grace has been given to us, we should extend that grace to others as well! We find all throughout the Bible that God always connected prayer and forgiveness. They are inseparable words! You cannot have one without the other!

# The Power of Confession and Forgiveness

Confessed sin and forgiveness tears down barriers that hinder our relationships with the LORD and one another! It opens up the doors of mercy and repairs the bridges that were once blocked by unforgiveness, anger and bitterness. These things are a stumbling block to a right relationship with the Lord and others. It hinders our blessings that God so much desires to give us. We cannot have hate, anger and bitterness toward our neighbor and expect God to bless us abundantly. We must strive diligently to walk in love and peace with men and our creator.

The Apostle Paul told the Corinthian believers: "Now whom you forgive anything, I also forgive. For if indeed I have forgiven anything, I have forgiven that one for your sakes in the presence of Christ, lest Satan should take advantage of us; for we are not ignorant of his devices." 2 Corinthians 2:10-11 NKJV

In other words, as we forgive, God forgives us. We must not be ignorant of Satan's devices. He is the hinderer of all blessings. He comes to steal, kill and destroy, but Jesus came that we might have life and have it more abundantly. John 10:10

In the Book of Hebrews 12:14-15 , the writer exhorts us to follow peace with all men and holiness, without which no man shall see the Lord. Looking diligently lest any man fail of the grace of God; lest any root of bitterness springing up trouble you, and thereby many be defiled. Unforgiveness gives us a hostile attitude, which eventually causes bitterness to spring up, defiling the one who is walking in unforgiveness. Sooner or later the heart then becomes hardened

# The Ultimate Example of Forgiveness

  Jesus Christ presented the ultimate example of grace and forgiveness even as he prepared to go to the cross to be crucified. In the Garden of Gethsemane, as Jesus was about to be arrested. The Bible records that Peter drew a sword and cut off the ear of a Roman soldier. Peter was in no mood for grace and forgiveness, but was ready to fight.  Yet we find the grace and forgiveness of  Jesus in Matt 26:51-54.

Matthew 26:51-54 NKJV
(51) And suddenly, one of those who were with Jesus stretched out his hand and drew his sword, struck the servant of the high priest, and cut off his ear.
(52) But Jesus said to him, "Put your sword in its place, for all who take the sword will perish by the sword.
(53) Or do you think that I cannot now pray to My Father, and He will provide Me with more than twelve legions of angels?
(54) How then could the Scriptures be fulfilled, that it must happen thus?"
 Jesus in the Garden of Gethsemane could have prayed to the Father and angels could have been released on his behalf to protect him, but instead he showed mercy, patience and forgiveness. Even when Jesus was beaten, lied on, crucified and hung on a cross,  he looked to the Father and said, "Father forgive them for they know not what they do."

"Then Jesus said, "Father, forgive them, for they do not know what they do." And they divided His garments and cast lots."
Luke 23:34 NKJV

This by all accounts must be the greatest example of forgiveness that has ever been shown in all the earth.

# The Apostle Paul's Disagreement

In the New Testament book of Acts 15, the Apostle Paul and Barnabas had a disagreement about taking John Mark on a missionary journey. The scripture says that they disagreed about him journeying with them and as a result there was a sharp contention.

Acts 15:36-41 NKJV
(36) Then after some days Paul said to Barnabas, "Let us now go back and visit our brethren in every city where we have preached the word of the Lord, and see how they are doing."
(37) Now Barnabas was determined to take with them John called Mark.
(38) But Paul insisted that they should not take with them the one who had departed from them in Pamphylia, and had not gone with them to the work.
**(39) Then the contention became so sharp that they parted from one another. And so, Barnabas took Mark and sailed to Cyprus;**
(40) but Paul chose Silas and departed, being commended by the brethren to the grace of God.
(41) And he went through Syria and Cilicia, strengthening the churches.

Can you imagine this? I am speaking about the Apostle Paul who wrote the majority of the New Testament books of the Bible by the Holy Spirit. He and fellow laborer Barnabas got into a big contention. The Bible says as a result they parted from one another. Brothers and Sisters, it does not matter who we are. We can all be offended in some way, but the question is not what caused the contention, but can we forgive one another after the contention!

The primary reason was because the Apostle Paul did not want to take John Mark on another missionary journey with him. (the writer of the Gospel of Mark)

Barnabas disagreed, because Barnabas and Mark were cousins. For some reason or another Mark had offended Paul, and Paul did not want him to go.  Many theologians say that John Mark had left him during one of their missionary campaigns while preaching the Gospel.

"Now when Paul and his party set sail from Paphos, they came to Perga in Pamphylia; and John, departing from them, returned to Jerusalem."
Acts 13:13 NKJV

So, John Mark left Paul for some reason. The Bible doesn't give us the reason, but Paul was offended by it and did not want Mark to accompany him again. The Bible says that the contention was so sharp that Paul and Barnabas separated one from another.   Did you get that? It was not just a small argument, but a sharp contention! We then read later in 2 Timothy 4: 11 that Paul speaks well about Mark.  Theologians believe this scripture shows there was forgiveness and reconciliation between Paul and Mark.

2 Timothy 4:9-11 NKJV
(9) Be diligent to come to me quickly;
(10) for Demas has forsaken me, having loved this present world, and has departed for Thessalonica-- Crescens for Galatia, Titus for Dalmatia.
(11) Only Luke is with me. Get Mark and bring him with you, for he is useful to me for ministry.
As Paul sits in prison, he writes the book of 2 Timothy and as he shares his heart, he tells Timothy to bring Mark with you, for he is useful to me for ministry.

**The Apostle Paul's Forgiveness**

In 1 Corinthians 5: 5, there was a man who had done some immoral things  in the church and Paul said to turn

the man over to Satan because of his trespasses.  Let'
read:

1 Corinthians 5:4-5 NKJV
(4) In the name of our Lord Jesus Christ, when you are
gathered together, along with my spirit, with the power
of our Lord Jesus Christ,
(5) deliver such a one to Satan for the destruction of the
flesh, that his spirit may be saved in the day of the Lord
Jesus.

In 2 Corinthians 2: 10-11, Paul forgives and releases the
man in the name of the LORD so that Satan would not
take advantage of the unforgiveness.
(10) Now whom you forgive anything, I also forgive. For
if indeed I have forgiven anything, I have forgiven that
one for your sakes in the presence of Christ,
(11) lest Satan should take advantage of us; for we are
not ignorant of his devices.

   Notice what he said in 2 Cor 2: 11, less Satan get
should take advantage of us we are not ignorant of his
devices. As the body of Christ, we should not be ignorant
of Satan's devices which are division, dissension,
discord, disagreement, disunity, and disunion.  When we
forgive one another, it prevents the enemy from accusing
and taking advantage of us.
   In other words, we must endeavor to keep the unity
of the spirit in the bond of peace. We must always have a
spirit of forgiveness and keep the devil out of our
churches, marriages, families, friendships and
relationships.  The problem today is that there is a spirit
of pride that does not want to submit, surrender and be
humble enough to say I was wrong, or I forgive and
release you.  Remember that forgiveness is not for the
other person, it is for you!  We cannot be spirit filled
people and have unforgiveness in our hearts!  We must
always forgive according to scripture so that we may be

partakers of his grace, favor and continual blessings!

## SCRIPTURES ON FORGIVENESS

Matthew 5:23-24 NKJV
23 Therefore if you offer your gift on the altar, and there remember that your brother has anything against you,
24 leave your gift there before the altar and go. First be reconciled to your brother, and then come and offer your gift.

Matthew 6:10-15 KJV
10  Thy kingdom come. Thy will be done in earth, as it is in heaven.
11  Give us this day our daily bread.
12  And forgive us our debts, as we forgive our debtors.
13  And lead us not into temptation, but deliver us from evil: For thine is the kingdom, and the power, and the glory, forever. Amen.
14  For if ye forgive men their trespasses, your heavenly Father will also forgive you:
15  But if ye forgive not men their trespasses, neither will your Father forgive your trespasses.

Matthew 18:32-35 NKJV
32 Then his lord, after he had called him, said to him, O wicked servant, I forgave you all that debt because you begged me.
33 Should you not also have pitied your fellow servant, even as I had pity on you?
34 And his lord was angry, and delivered him to the tormentors until he should pay all that was due to him.
35 So likewise shall My heavenly Father do also to you, unless each one of you from your hearts forgive his brother their trespasses.

# CHAPTER 8 - UNREPENTANCE

As we prepare to discuss the last hindrance to the blessings of God, let's define what repentance is. Repentance in the Bible denotes a sense of guilt, an apprehension of God's mercy, sorrow for sin, and a turning away from sin unto God. It denotes a change of mind and conversion.

A good example of repentance can be compared to an individual taking a trip on a long road and going in the wrong direction. When they finally come to the conclusion that they are traveling on the wrong road that leads to hell, they get off at the next exit; Salvation in Jesus Name. You then take the road, Saved by Grace to Faith Lane which is a straight one-way road. You will then be traveling in the right direction to destiny and purpose.

This is an interesting way to look at repentance, but how many of us have ever been taking a trip on a road and we make a wrong turn and end up traveling in the wrong direction. Some of us have navigators or google maps, and as we listen to the directions, the electronic voice says turn right, turn left and we just keep on going.

Some of us even got human voices in the car, normally it's someone in the car (my wife) who keeps saying, "I think we are going the wrong way, and sometimes we ignore it!" How many of us know that the Holy Spirit is just like that little navigator voice or human voice! Many times, the Holy Spirit is speaking to our hearts and telling us the right thing to do but we ignore it. We must be extremely careful that we do not ignore the directions and instructions that the LORD gives us.

The Bible says in Proverbs 16:25, "There is a way that seems right to a man, but its end is the way of death." Can you imagine living your life a certain way believing that your way is the right way, and in the end you meet the LORD and find out it was the way of death?

This is exactly what happens to an unrepentant person. They believe and act in a way that says my way is the right way. It is also believing that sinful behavior is acceptable before God, therefore I have nothing to repent of. Unfortunately, this is not what the scripture teaches. The Bible clearly says in 2 Peter 3: 9:

"The Lord is not slack concerning his promise, as some men count slackness; but is longsuffering to us-ward, not willing that any should perish, but that all should come to repentance." (2 Peter 3:9)

In other words, God loves us so much that he desires that men and women would repent of their sins and come to him. Why? Because he loves us so much that he does not want anyone to perish or go to hell. Hell was not created for humans; it was created for the devil and his angels.

Jesus made mention of this in Matthew 25: 41, "Then shall he say also unto them on the left hand, Depart from me, ye cursed, into everlasting fire, prepared for the devil and his angels."

One of the most familiar passages of scripture is 2 Chron 7: 14 that says, "If my people who are called by my name, would humble themselves and pray, and seek my face and turn from their wicked ways, then will I hear from heaven and forgive their sins, and will heal their land."

This is very profound scripture that deals with repentance. God was telling Solomon that if he shuts up heaven because of the sin of the people and sends no rain, or commands the locust to devour the land, or sends pestilence among the people (2 Chron 7: 13) , he would move quickly on their behalf if they did one thing, and that is repent!

So, we see that calling on the name of the Lord, humility, prayer, seeking the face of God, and turning from our wicked ways will move God, and in response he will forgive sin and heal the land. Now I want you to think about what would happen if there was unrepentance! There would be no rain, the locusts would devour the land, and pestilence would be among the people.

This is why unrepentance is detrimental to our wellbeing and spiritual growth. God is moved by repentant hearts, surrender and submission. Repentance deals with humility. Unrepentance is a result of pride, and pride is an abomination in the sight of the LORD. All of the hindrances to the blessings of God that have been discussed in previous chapters can be resolved by humbling ourselves and repenting of disobedience, idolatry, pride, rebellion, unbelief and unforgiveness.

There is nowhere in the Bible that I can find where anyone who walked in one of these spiritual hindrances walked in the blessings and favor of the LORD! In the book of Matthew, we find that the message of John the Baptist was a plain message. He didn't have a lot of sermons. His simple message was:

"In those days came John the Baptist, preaching in the wilderness of Judaea, and saying, Repent ye: for the kingdom of heaven is at hand." Matthew 3:1-2

We also find in the book of Matthew that Jesus came on the scene preaching the same message: "From that time Jesus began to preach, and to say, Repent: for the kingdom of heaven is at hand." Matthew 4:17

The Kingdom of heaven literally means that the King of Kings and Lord of Lords is here to reestablish the Kingdom of God over the rebellious part of God's creation, which is planet earth. It refers to the Messiah's Kingdom on earth. Jesus came to reestablish the Kingdom of God on earth. In the very beginning Adam was supposed to establish Gods Kingdom on earth and failed because of his disobedience and sin.

Sin is what hinders the blessing of God in every person's life. Sin causes men to worship false gods, which is idolatry. It causes men to walk in pride, arrogance and self-righteousness, it causes men to rebel against God's established authority, and it causes men to walk in fear, doubt and unbelief. It causes people to walk in unforgiveness against their neighbor because of offense or hardness of heart.

Even in the book of Acts 2:38, the Apostle Peter preached and said, "Repent, and let every one of you be baptized in the name of Jesus Christ for the remission of sins; and you shall receive the gift of the Holy Spirit."

Do you see a pattern in the scriptures? The message of repentance was the Kingdom message. Brother and sisters, this message has not changed. Why? Because there will always be people in the world that need the saving grace of Jesus Christ.

We live in a time where people have become desensitized to sin, evil, and ungodliness. The people of God should never become desensitized to sin, and we should never conform to the pattern of this world and allow sinful nature to become a lifestyle.

We should always let our light shine as beacons of light that draw others to Jesus Christ. Because when people see you, they see Jesus. If you engage in questionable behavior or speech, it does not bring glory to the Father in Heaven. Repentance restores our relationship to God. Repentance wipes the slate clean.

## The Apostle Paul Speaks about Repentance

The Apostle Paul also spoke about repentance as well in Acts 17: 30-31.

Acts 17:30-31
(30) And the times of this ignorance God winked at, but now commands all men everywhere to repent:
(31) Because he hath appointed a day, in which he will judge the world in righteousness by that man whom he hath ordained; whereof he hath given assurance unto all men, in that he hath raised him from the dead.

There are two types of repentance; one for the believer and the unbeliever.
If a believer sins, he goes before Father God with godly sorrow in the Name of Jesus confessing their sin, repenting of their sin, and asking forgiveness of sins.

If you are an unbeliever who has not accepted Jesus Christ as Lord and Savior, you must be born again. You must confess your sins, repent of your sins, and then according to Romans 10:9, "That if you confess with your mouth the Lord Jesus, and believe in your heart that God has raised Him from the dead, you will be saved."

An unrepentant person cannot please God, and the only prayer that God desires to hear from an unbeliever is a prayer of repentance. Repentance is important because the Bible says that we have all sinned and fallen short of the glory of God.

"As it is written, There is none righteous, no, not one. There is none that understands, there is none that seeks after God." Romans 3:10-11

"For all have sinned, and come short of the glory of God." Romans 3:23

Because of unrighteousness and sin, the LORD has made a way for our salvation, but we must acknowledge our sin before God so that he can forgive us.

1 John 1:5-10 KJV
(5) This then is the message which we have heard of him, and declare unto you, that God is light, and in him is no darkness at all.
(6) If we say that we have fellowship with him, and walk in darkness, we lie, and do not the truth:
(7) But if we walk in the light, as he is in the light, we have fellowship one with another, and the blood of Jesus Christ his Son cleanses us from all sin.
(8) If we say that we have no sin, we deceive ourselves, and the truth is not in us.
(9) If we confess our sins, he is faithful and just to forgive us our sins, and to cleanse us from all unrighteousness.
(10) If we say that we have not sinned, we make him a liar, and his word is not in us.

There are three words that can help us remember what repentance is all about. It is the acronym CAT. It simply means confess, ask and thanks.

**Confess** – Honestly confess your sins, faults, failures, rebelliousness, disobedience and guilt for your sins.

**Ask** - first for forgiveness and cleansing. Ask God for self-discipline in overcoming problems and challenges. Ask for victory over bitterness, resentment, jealousy, greed, anger and ask for forgiveness if you have hurt others.

**Thank** God for his saving grace - Thank him for his forgiveness and presence in your life. Thank him for his help and his comfort with daily struggles, and remember to fill your mind with God's Word, and daily prayer. Always keep a clear conscience before God. Don't let a day go without confessing your sin or asking forgiveness of someone you may have offended.

"He who covers his sins will not prosper, but whoever confesses and forsakes them will have mercy."
Proverbs 28:13 NKJV

When we confess our sins, God releases grace and mercy in our lives to move forward without condemnation. The Bible says in Prov 28: 13 that a person who covers his sins will not prosper. This is exactly what this book is all about, removing hindrances to spiritual growth and the blessings that the LORD desires to release over our lives.

The question is, "Why would anyone want to cover or hide their sins?" If God is omniscient and all knowing, isn't it wise to confess and forsake our sins so that we can obtain mercy? The LORD desires to bless his people abundantly, but the condition is repentance, or a turning away from sin unto God. Repentance denotes a change of mind and conversion.

## Jeremiah Speaks about Repentance

In the books of Jeremiah, the LORD speaks prophetically about the people of God as it relates to sin and unrepentance. Let's take a look at Jeremiah 8:4-7:

(4) "Moreover, you shall say to them, 'thus says the LORD: "Will they fall and not rise? Will one turn away and not return?

(5) Why have this people slidden back, Jerusalem, in a perpetual backsliding? They hold fast to deceit; they refuse to return.

(6) I listened and heard, but they do not speak aright. No man repented of his wickedness, Saying, 'What have I done?' Everyone turned to his own course, as the horse rushes into the battle.

(7) "Even the stork in the heavens knows her appointed times; and the turtledove, the swift, and the swallow observe the time of their coming, but my people do not know the judgment of the LORD.

The LORD appears to be conversing with Jeremiah about the state of the people, and asks some interesting questions about repentance. Look at verse 4. Will they fall and not rise?" Will one turn away and not return? He goes on to ask a question in verse 5, why has Jerusalem slid back in a perpetual backsliding? They hold fast to their deceit and refuse to return.

Even their conversations grieve the LORD. Look at verse 6. No one speaks aright and no man repented of his wickedness, saying what have I done? It is clear that the LORD desires that they would repent of their sins but they are in a state of unrepentance!

The LORD even says, everyone turned to his own course as a horse rushes into battle. (Verse 6) This is amazing! What the LORD is saying is because of their hardened hearts they are in an unrepentant state and refuse to turn from their sin. In other words, they are in a state of unrepentance.

The LORD then said that even the birds know the seasons and appointed times to do what is right. Yet, the people of God do not know or discern the times, seasons and judgement of the Lord.

Beloved, why it is that man refuses to acknowledge his sin and shortcomings before the LORD? Repentance is the key to restoration in Jesus Name. If we fall short, we should be quick to repent of our sins, so that we our relationship with the LORD can be restored. This is God's way of restoration when we fall short.

If you offend your brother or sister, be quick to repent. If you sin against the LORD, be quick to repent. The difference between King Saul and King David is that David acknowledged his sin, was quick to repent, and prayed with a pure heart for restoration.
Psalm 51 was written as a result of this. God loves us so much and desires to bless his people, but we must never get comfortable with sin. Every hindrance that we have discussed in this book can be resolved by simply acknowledging, confessing and repenting of our sin.

## SCRIPTURES ON REPENTANCE

Matthew 11:20-22 NKJV
(20) Then He began to rebuke the cities in which most of His mighty works had been done, because they did not repent:
(21) "Woe to you, Chorazin! Woe to you, Bethsaida! For if the mighty works which were done in you had been done in Tyre and Sidon, they would have repented long ago in sackcloth and ashes.
(22) But I say to you, it will be more tolerable for Tyre and Sidon in the Day of Judgment than for you.

Matthew 21:32 KJV
(32) For John came unto you in the way of righteousness, and ye believed him not, but the publicans and the harlots believed him: and you, when ye had seen it, repented not afterward, that you might believe him.

Luke 13:1-5 NKJV
(1) There were present at that season some who told Him about the Galileans whose blood Pilate had mingled with their sacrifices.
(2) And Jesus answered and said to them, "Do you suppose that these Galileans were worse sinners than all other Galileans, because they suffered such things?
(3) I tell you, no; but unless you repent you will all likewise perish.
(4) Or those eighteen on whom the tower in Siloam fell and killed them, do you think that they were worse sinners than all other men who dwelt in Jerusalem?
(5) I tell you, no; but unless you repent you will all likewise perish."

Acts 17:30-31 NKJV
(30) Truly, these times of ignorance God overlooked, but now commands all men everywhere to repent,
(31) Because He has appointed a day on which He will judge the world in righteousness by the Man whom He has ordained. He has given assurance of this to all by raising Him from the dead."

Revelation 2:5 NKJV
(5) Remember therefore from where you have fallen; repent and do the first works, or else I will come to you quickly and remove your lampstand from its place-- unless you repent.

Revelation 16:8-11 NKJV
(8) Then the fourth angel poured out his bowl on the sun, and power was given to him to scorch men with fire.
(9) And men were scorched with great heat, and they blasphemed the name of God who has power over these plagues; and they did not repent and give Him glory.
(10) Then the fifth angel poured out his bowl on the throne of the beast, and his kingdom became full of darkness; and they gnawed their tongues because of the

pain.

(11) They blasphemed the God of heaven because of their pains and their sores, and did not repent of their deeds.

**Jesus Christ the Perfect Example**

There are so many examples in the Bible of men and women who were blessed and favored in the Lord. These were Saints that loved, served and were faithful to God. Some of those examples are:

Abel who offered an excellent sacrifice to God (Gen 4: 4, Heb 11: 4)

Enoch who walked with God (Gen 5: 24)

Noah who was perfect in his generation (Gen 6: 9)

Abraham who was called the friend of God (2 Chron 20: 7, James 2: 23)

Joseph who was a man of integrity and type of Christ (Gen 37:3, Gen 39: 2-4)

Moses who spoke with God as a man speaks to friend face to face (Exo 33: 11)

King Josiah who pleased the LORD (2 Kings 22: 2)

King David, who was a man after God's own heart (Acts 13: 22)

Daniel who had an excellent spirit and no error or fault was found in him (Dan 6: 1-4)

Jabez was more honorable than his brothers (2 Chron 4: 9-10)

John the Disciple that Jesus loved. (John 21: 20-22)

Hannah who God gave favor and birthed the mighty Prophet Samuel (1 Sam 1: 20)

Esther who was favored by the LORD and saved the Hebrew people (Est 2: 17)

Ruth who married Boaz, and was the Great Grandmother of King David (Ruth 4: 10)

Mary was blessed, favored by God and birthed the Savior Jesus Christ (Luk 1: 30-33)

And last but certainly not least, Jesus Christ who was the only begotten Son of God, Savior of the world, King of

Kings, and LORD of Lord's who was a servant of all, died for us all, and is an example to all!

"For to this you were called, because Christ also suffered for us, leaving us an example, that you should follow His steps: "Who committed no sin, nor was deceit found in his mouth."
1 Peter 2:21-22 NKJV

If you have not accepted Jesus Christ as Lord and Savior, I implore you to repent of your sins, renounce every evil deed and thought, and turn to Jesus Christ for salvation.

Roman 10: 9-10 that says:
(9) that if you confess with your mouth the Lord Jesus and believe in your heart that God has raised Him from the dead, you will be saved.
(10) For with the heart one believes unto righteousness, and with the mouth confession is made unto salvation.
Jesus said in John 3: 3, "Most assuredly, I say to you, unless one is born again, he cannot see the kingdom of God."
John 3:3 NKJV

Peter said in 2 Peter 3: 9, "God is not willing that any should perish, but that all would come to repentance."

Beloved, God has a plan for your life and desires to do great things in you and through you. Not only that, but God desires to give you abundant life which will only happen when you repent of your sins, and accept Jesus Christ as LORD and Savior.
**Here is how you can receive Christ and be assured of your eternity:**

1. Admit your need (I am a sinner).
2. Be willing to turn from your sins (Repent of your sins).
3. Pray and believe in your heart and confess with your

mouth that Jesus Christ is Lord. (Believe and receive Jesus Christ as Lord and Savior)
4. Be baptized in the Name of Jesus for the remission of your sins and you shall receive the gift of the Holy Spirit. (Be filled with the Holy Spirit)

How to Pray:
Heavenly Father, I come to you in the Name of Jesus, I am a sinner and I repent of my sins. I believe in my heart and confess with my mouth that Jesus is Lord. I believe that you died on the cross for my sins. You were buried and resurrected on the third day. Come into my heart and life. Purge me and fill me with your precious Holy Spirit. Today I believe, trust and follow Jesus Christ as my Lord and Savior. In Jesus Name. Amen.

This is just the beginning of a wonderful new life in Jesus Christ. To deepen this relationship, you should:

Read your Bible every day to know Christ better. Communicate and talk to God in prayer every day. Tell others about Christ. Worship, fellowship, and serve with other born-again Spirit filled Christians in a church where Christ, and the true Gospel is preached. As Christ's representative in the world, demonstrate your new life by your love and concern for others. The Bible says, "Let your light so shine, that others may see your good works and glorify your Father in heaven. Matt 5: 16.

# References

Mandingo, Og. *The Greatest Salesman in the World*. New York F. Fell, 1963.

Rutland, Mark. *Nevertheless*. Lake Mary, FL: Charisma House, 2001.

Bevere, John. *Under Cover: The Promise of Protection under His Authority*. Thomas Nelson, 2001.

Strong, James. *The New Strong's Exhaustive Concordance of the Bible: With Main Concordance, Appendix to the Main Concordance, Hebrew and Aramaic Dictionary of the Old Testament, Greek Dictionary of the New Testament*. Nashville: T. Nelson, 1997.

"Dictionary, Encyclopedia and Thesaurus." *The Free Dictionary*. Accessed October 22, 2018. http://www.thefreedictionary.com/.

"American Dictionary of the English Language." Webster's Dictionary 1828. Accessed November 05, 2018. http://webstersdictionary1828.com/.

Meyers, Rick. *"E-Sword: Bible Study for the PC."* E-Sword. 2016. Accessed August 08, 2016. http://www.e-sword.net/.

# About the Author

Pastor Jamal E. Quinn is the Senior Pastor of Firm Foundation Christian Fellowship in Riverview, FL. He is a native of Louisville, Kentucky and a U.S. Navy veteran of 21 years.

He accepted the call into the ministry and was licensed as a Minister of the Gospel of Jesus Christ in 1999. In May 2002 - 2003, while serving in the military he was ordered to the Middle East with Special Operations Command Central Forward on a one-year assignment in Doha, Qatar. It was at this time in the desert, that the Lord called him to preach the Gospel and minister the Word of God in True Righteousness, Holiness, Deliverance and Truth.

In June 2003, he was assigned to Naval Air Station Jacksonville, Florida on another assignment. During this time, he committed himself to a thorough and diligent study of the Holy Bible. In September of 2005, he retired after serving 21 years in the U.S. Navy.

In Oct 2005, he returned home to Riverview, Florida where the Lord led him to start a community Bible study by faith. Preaching and teaching the Gospel in his neighborhood to anyone that had an ear to hear. In Oct 2007, after faithfully conducting a Bible study group in his home, the Lord called Pastor Jamal and Prophetess Sheryl Quinn to plant Firm Foundation Christian Fellowship in the community of Riverview.

Pastor Quinn is a visionary, shepherd, and watchman who preaches the Gospel of the Kingdom with passion, power and truth. Pastor Quinn's passion is teaching, exhorting and encouraging the Body of Christ to fulfill their God ordained destiny, and to live their lives as examples in Jesus Christ.

He received his Associate of Science Degree at Excelsior College, Albany, New York, and obtained his Bachelor of Arts in Pastoral Ministry from South Florida Bible College and Theological Seminary in Deerfield Beach, FL.

For additional information on Pastor Quinn or other books, visit https://jamalquinn.com/ or email jamq9@verizon.net

For additional information on Firm Foundation Christian Fellowship, visit https://www.firmfoundationcf.org